Father Hunger

Father Hunger

Why God Calls Men to Love and Lead Their Families

Douglas Wilson

THOMAS NELSON
Since 1798

NASHVILLE DALLAS MEXICO CITY RIO DE JANEIRO

© 2012 by Douglas James Wilson

All rights reserved. No portion of this book may be reproduced, stored in a retrieval system, or transmitted in any form or by any means—electronic, mechanical, photocopy, recording, scanning, or other—except for brief quotations in critical reviews or articles, without the prior written permission of the publisher.

Published in Nashville, Tennessee, by Thomas Nelson. Thomas Nelson is a registered trademark of Thomas Nelson, Inc.

Thomas Nelson, Inc., titles may be purchased in bulk for educational, business, fund-raising, or sales promotional use. For information, please e-mail SpecialMarkets@ThomasNelson.com.

Unless otherwise noted, Scripture quotations are taken from THE ENGLISH STANDARD VERSION®. Copyright ©2001 by Crossway Bibles, a division of Good News Publishers.

Scripture quotations marked KJV are from the King James Version.

Italics in Scripture quotations reflect the author's added emphasis.

Library of Congress Cataloging-in-Publication Data

Wilson, Douglas, 1953-
Father hunger : why God calls men to love and lead their families / Douglas Wilson.
p. cm.
Includes bibliographical references (p.) and index.
ISBN 978-1-59555-476-5
1. Fatherhood--Religious aspects--Christianity. 2. Fathers--Religious life. I. Title.
BV4529.17.W557 2012
248.8'421--dc23

Printed in the United States of America

12 13 14 15 QG 6 5 4 3 2 1

For James Irwin Wilson, a true father.
This book is dedicated to him, a man I have respected as long as I can remember, and as deep as I go.

"Grandchildren are the crown of the aged,
and the glory of children is their fathers."
—Proverbs 17:6

Contents

Chapter 1

First Words

I once heard a conference speaker make a profound point in passing, a point that has stayed with me in the years since.[1] He said that the first recorded words spoken by a human being were the words spoken by Adam when the Lord presented his wife to him. When Adam first spoke, it was in response to a woman, and the words he spoke were poetry. We really need to learn how to take more careful notice of those "opening words."

We should pay special attention also to the first words spoken by the Father of Jesus Christ at the beginning of the New Testament. We know from all of Scripture that God is the Father of Jesus Christ—He is God the *Father,* after all—but these opening words tell us a great deal about what this archetypal fatherhood is like.

> And when Jesus was baptized, immediately he went up from the water, and behold, the heavens were opened to him, and he saw the Spirit of God descending like a dove and coming to rest on him; and behold, a voice from heaven said, "This is my beloved Son, with whom I am well pleased." (Matt. 3:16–17)

There is a world of information about fatherhood in these two brief verses. First, when Jesus was baptized, His Father was *there*. Second, He made His presence *felt* by sending His Spirit to descend like a dove in order to rest upon Jesus. Third, He made His presence *known* by speaking. And so what did He say? His statement corresponded with the giving of the Spirit in that the Father identified with His Son. He said, "This is my Son." Fourth, He expressed His love for His Son—"This is my *beloved* Son." And last, He expressed His *pleasure* in His Son. The first thing we are told about the relationship of the Father to the Son is that the Father thought His Son was doing a great job.

So this is what fatherhood is like. This is where fatherhood reaches its ultimate expression. In human history, there will never be a more perfect father-and-son moment than this moment between Father and Son. This is the keynote—pleasure. This is the pitch that a father/son relationship needs to match—"well pleased."

When we don't match that pitch, a lot of things start going wrong. In fact, so many things start going wrong that we sometimes miss the source of all the trouble. In our generation we are confronted with many social dislocations that all go back to a foundational father hunger. All men are the son of some man, and all women are the daughter of some man, but far too many of them have never heard their father say anything like what the Father said to His Son.

Well pleased is an alien concept to many of us, and because it is so unknown, we have a great deal of cultural debris to work through. That being the case, we should perhaps get started.

As we look around, we know that *we* are broken, but we somehow assume that our notions of fatherhood are intact. But perhaps it goes the other way. Perhaps our world is as broken as it is because our understanding of fatherhood was shattered first. Mike Wilkerson puts it this way:

> Tragically, for many of us the Father-child relationship is fraught with fear, shame, dread, disappointment, or absence. For some of us . . . the word *father* has been darkened by the worst evils. Can you ever hope to know God as your Father if your view of *father* is so broken?[2]

But this problem can be turned around, and should be turned around. Our understanding of fathers, and our subsequent understanding of everything else, cannot be put right until we rediscover the Father. This is not written for unbelievers alone. There are many professing Christians who are emotional atheists. "We may hold onto orthodox ideas about [the Father], but our hearts disconnect," says Wilkerson; "our affection cools; we just don't trust him."[3] We assume too readily that it is impossible for us to turn back to the face of the Father, but there actually is good news for people just like us.

Like the father in the story that Jesus told about the prodigal son, He is looking down the road for us.

Chapter 2

What Fathers Are For

After being introduced to the principles that undergird this book, one young father once exclaimed, "Now I know what I am *for*!" Fatherhood is not some optional add-on extra, but rather is something *central,* not just to a well-adjusted suburban family with all the white picket fence trimmings, but to all things in heaven and on earth. Fathers really do matter.

Much of what will be argued throughout the course of this book will not seem very enlightened or progressive to today's average reader, and so we must begin by addressing the problems created by something called *egalitarianism.* We shouldn't be put off by this elongated word—we all know plenty of other big words that don't bother us, like *delicatessen* or *basketball. Egalitarianism* simply means "equalism," and like a number of other similar words, the poison in that word is found in the *ism.*

Now of course we know and agree that there is an important sense in which we are all supposed to be treated as equals. In a court of law, for example, we know that the rules governing admissible evidence should not vary in accordance with the income bracket of the defendant. And this kind of equality in our human courts is, at its best, a reflection of the equality we can expect to find before the throne of God on the final Day of Judgment. Blondes will not get favored treatment there, and neither will men who graduated from an Ivy League school. That boyish grin that got you through so many scrapes as a young man will have lost a good deal of its persuasive charm.

And in the same way, but on the flip side, the salvation that is offered in Christ knows no rank or station. God saves kings and Pharisees, women and laboring men, white men and black women, slaves and aristocrats. In Christ, as Paul famously says, there is neither Jew nor Greek, male or female, slave or free (Gal. 3:28). There is obviously an important kind of "equality" here as well, and no truehearted Christian should ever be suspicious of it.

So in what sense can "equality" ever be bad? In what sense, then, is egalitarianism a "poison"? A moment's reflection should show how a mistake here could be very easy to make. From hearing that someone from group X and someone else from group Y should be *treated* the same in a court of law, someone might easily buy into the notion that members of these two groups must actually *be* the same. But they are manifestly different. A child is different from a woman, who differs from a man.

When two things are the same we tend to treat them the same. But if we treat two things the same, it does not follow that they *are* the same. If we found two hammers on the workbench, we wouldn't have any trouble picking up either one of them to do the job—because we intend to treat them exactly the same. But it does not follow from this that if we should treat something the same (in a legal setting) they must, therefore, *be* the same. A man might be called up to take care of all his tools, treating them all with the *same* kind of respect. But treating a hammer with respect and a screwdriver with respect means treating them differently—you don't twist screws with a hammer, and you don't try to drive nails with the handle of a screwdriver.

If people are different, in order to get them all into the same good equality zone, you must treat them differently. Moreover, in different sorts of situations, you must do this differently. When people are different, and you treat them just the same in *every* circumstance, then you will get some very different, and very inequitable, results.

Now, what does this have to do with fathers? In order for a man and a woman to enjoy the same good marriage, they must each fulfill very different roles. The same good marriage requires one man and one woman, who are, let us admit, two very different ingredients. In order to get the same result of "a good tight fit," I must treat the nut and the bolt differently. Both nut and bolt enjoy being part of the same function, but in order for this to happen, they must also enjoy performing completely different functions. They cannot enjoy doing the same thing together unless they enjoy doing completely different things . . . together.

So in order for a father to *be* a father, it is necessary for him to embrace (as a good thing) the reality that God has appointed us all to very different roles, and that He has configured us—body, soul, and spirit—in line with those appointments. A man is called to be a father *all the way down*. His fatherhood taps into something much deeper and much more profound than some of his accidental features—the fact that he was born in St. Louis, or has blue eyes or sandy brown hair.

If a man were to lose a finger, he is still the same man, minus the finger. If he were to go bald, the same thing is true. But we cannot "unfather" him without removing him from every relationship he has, and this has the effect of annihilating him. Our personal identity is established by our relationships, and this involves far more than our geographical relationships (e.g., "to the left of"). I am not just standing north of my daughter; I am a *father* to my daughter. That cannot be undone without undoing both of us. It actually cannot be done at all, fortunately, but a lot of damage has been caused because people have come to *think* that it can be done. They think that fatherhood is an accidental feature, separable from what the man is deep down. Just as birth control has radically altered the modern understanding of a man's responsibility for his progeny, so also has it altered our understanding of a man's identity being wrapped up in his progeny. We have come to believe that this identity of fatherhood is susceptible to a few redefinitions, or to a few more progressive court cases.

This is all done in the name of diversity. But when we don't accept God's creation design, we have no reason to respect diversity, or anything else, for that matter. Fatherhood is one of the disrespected rejects.[1]

I recall reading a sample of this kind of feminist reductionism several decades ago, and the author was arguing how silly and arbitrary it all seemed to her. Her example was about when a man and woman are in bed together, and they hear an odd noise outside the house. Why, she asked, do we say that "the one with the penis" has to be the one to go and check on the noise? But is that all we are talking about? A "rock, paper, scissors" way of making decisions? Is it really that simplistic?

The role of a father as a provider and protector is not an arbitrary assignment given to an arbitrarily selected group, regardless of any other consideration. Here is the mandate given to Adam (Gen. 2:15)—God wants men both to work and to protect. Work has to do with nurture and cultivation, while protection refers to a man's duty to be a fortress for his family.[2] We find a working definition of masculinity in the first few pages of the Bible.[3]

When men take up their responsibilities to nurture and cultivate, and to protect and guard the fruit of that nurture and cultivation, they are doing something that resonates with their foundational, creational nature. When they walk away from these responsibilities, in a very real sense they are—don't miss this—*walking away from their assigned masculine identity.*

If the Scriptures teach that we are fearfully and wonderfully made, as they most certainly do (Ps. 139:14), there is no reason to believe that this glorious intricacy attends only one-tenth of the project (say in the assembly of the DNA), with everything else being done in a spirit of careless slapdashery. The assigned roles given to fathers are as intricately fitted to the reality of his broader relationships as the intricacy of the mechanics of reproduction itself. To think differently is to believe that the engineer who designed the dashboard so marvelously just decided to throw a jumble of parts together when it came to the engine under the hood, in the hope that it would somehow magically work. There is no reason to think a person would ever do such a thing. No, God is a *precision* engineer. The work that went into the interior is seen also in the engine block, and then in the drive train, and so on.

I used the phrase "provider and protector" a moment ago. This is not something we came up with ourselves as a pragmatic solution to certain practical problems. It is not a human invention or tradition, or just a holdover from our hunter/gatherer days. This is an essential part of God's creation design. When we look at the beginning of our race, looking carefully at our circumstances when God placed us in the world, we see these roles *assigned* to the man. Again, men were put into this world in order to work it and to keep it. They were placed here with this twofold mandate in mind. This is what men are *for*.[4]

All men are called, like Adam our first father, to provide for their families and to protect their families. Christians believe that the universe was created, and further, we believe that it is designed all the way through and all the way down. This created reality encompasses every atom, every hair, every leaf, and every man, woman, and child. The man was fitted for his task, and the task was fitted for the man. If God prepares good works beforehand for all of us to walk in (Eph. 2:10), then doesn't it stand to reason that He prepares tasks that are suited to our sex? Men don't carry things because they happen to have broad shoulders. They have broad shoulders because God created them to carry things.

All this is to say that fatherhood has a *point,* and that the point goes far beyond the services provided by a stud farm or a fertilization clinic. Fatherhood has a point that extends far beyond the moment of begetting. That point extends into everything, and if we are baffled by what the point might be, wisdom might dictate that we should read the manual—the Scriptures God gave to us. But modernists want to keep that intricate device we call fathers and, when stumped, consult a different manual entirely. This is akin to troubleshooting problems with your Apple laptop by consulting the Chilton manual for a '72 Ford pickup truck. And we wonder why our families are not getting on better.

This might be a good place to add—for it must be added somewhere—that to write a book on why "fathers really matter" is *not* to imply that mothers don't. Because these issues have become so politicized in our day, it has been easy for those who have a contrary view to rush to attack a caricature of what is actually being said. What is being argued here is that fatherhood has a point, not that motherhood doesn't. My point is that masculinity is crucial, not that femininity is superfluous. To say that Dad is indispensable is not to say that you can drop Mom any old time. As C. S. Lewis might have had Professor Kirke say, were he here, "Logic! Bless me, what *do* they teach them in these schools?" A person should be able to write a book arguing that Vitamin D is an important component of a person's health without being accused of making a vicious and unwarranted attack on Vitamin E.

This has become more difficult because the feminists have, in their typically humorless way,[5] politicized the green fields of human sexuality, turning everything a light and very dry brown. Where there used to be rich harvests, we now have a famine. Let us call it the "faminine mystique."

Egalitarianism wants to say, when confronted with something that Scripture says a father should take responsibility for, that the arrangement is "not fair." Why shouldn't the mother be the breadwinner? Why shouldn't the man be the one to submit to his spouse? Of course, in one sense, it is not fair. But it is *good*.[6] Part of that goodness is found in the realization that the Bible teaches that wives are to submit to their *own* husbands, and not to men generally. Because of this submission in the context of each family, and not in the context of bureaucracies and federal agencies, a textured and complicated relationship between the sexes will develop in society at large. It will not be flat and egalitarian, but it will be good.[7]

We are all of us finite, and this means that we can't be two (or more) creatures at once. And if God determined to create some very different kinds of creatures—as a quick glance at possums and seraphim, pebbles from the driveway and moons around Jupiter, wolf spiders and Vegas fan dancers will confirm that He did—then this means that any one of these creatures can't be another one of them. God said to each of us not only that we should "be," but also that we should "be *this*." But being a finite *this* entails not being a whole bunch of other *thats*. I cannot simultaneously be a plumber in Duluth and a pine tree in Nova Scotia.[8]

Moreover, not one of these variegated creatures has any ground for complaint. God could have made every creature just exactly the same, all of us round and shiny like little ball bearings one centimeter across, with all the invisible serial numbers distinguishing us one from another hidden away in the decrees and secret counsels of God. And there we would all be, pretty much all of us really bored.

But what He actually did was make the gaudiest show *ever,* which started at the beginning of our story when Adam looked at Eve for the first time and, as already noted, started speaking poetry.

So this word *unfair* has to be examined, just like the word *equality.* It would not be fair to convict me in a murder trial on trumped-up, inconsistent, and contradictory evidence, and it is also not fair (*obviously,* right?) that I don't have wings to enable me to take short, refreshing flights on Sunday afternoons when the weather is pleasant. But surely the former use has to be recognized as different from the latter? The former points to a genuine injustice, and the latter points to someone who spent too much time daydreaming in his youth.

There is true glory for a man in accepting his assigned place, and doing so in all humility. For a father to recognize that God has assigned him a particular role is not arrogance. Neither is it pride when he picks up his responsibilities. There *is* hubris when a glow worm thinks he is supposed to be a supernova, when a prince strives to be a pauper, and when a man thinks he is supposed to be a woman—or almost as bad, a sorry excuse for a man. We see the same problem when a biological father neglects his obligation to be a real father. But what does that mean exactly?

Generational Importance

To answer that question fully, we have to consider the *generational* importance of fathers. A common expression for dying in Scripture is the image of falling asleep. But less noticed is the image found frequently in the book of Genesis, and that is the image of being gathered to your people. The death of Abraham is described this way (Gen. 25:8), as well as that of Ishmael (Gen. 25:17), Isaac (Gen. 35:29), and Jacob (Gen. 49:33).

God's people are not just united in spirit with those who happen to be currently alive. Our union in Christ extends upstream to our fathers and far downstream to our sons. The communion of saints is not chronologically bound. And so when we speak of fathers and sons, we should not limit this to those fathers and sons whom we have happened to meet.

We have a (very modern) tendency to view each quarter of a generation as a separate pond. We gather around this pond (called the eighties) until it is time to move, and we find ourselves living around another pond called the nineties. Each decade seems to take on its own personality, a process admittedly made easier to identify by time-bound artifacts like disco and lava lamps. But Scripture teaches us that all our generations are *connected* to one another—humanity is more like a river than a series of ponds. Of course, a river changes course, narrows and widens, and bends in ways that make it impossible to see upstream or downstream very far. But it is a river nonetheless, and everything upstream affects us now, just as everything we are doing will affect those downstream from us.

To take a very simple example, why do we have sixty seconds in a minute and sixty minutes in an hour? Why are there 360 degrees in a circle? The answer is that the ancient Sumerians, the first literate culture that we have artifacts from, had a numerical system that operated on a base-60 level, unlike ours, which is base-10.[9] That is a long way upstream, but every time you look at your watch, you are paying silent homage to some stargazer named Iphur-kishi. Or perhaps it was a bean counter named Zababa-il.

If human culture is in fact a river, and yet our experience of it is very much like living on a pond because we can't go upstream at all, and can only go downstream from our birth for eighty years or so, how are we to deal with this? The quick answer is that we are to trust God—trust God when He teaches us that history is a river, and trust Him when He tells us how to faithfully live on our stretch of it. This is the difference between trying to control or steer history ourselves, and trying to cooperate with the one who actually does so. Trust God, and obey, and leave the consequences to Him. He knows our limitations.

> *As a father shows compassion to his children,*
> *so the Lord shows compassion to those who fear him.*
> *For he knows our frame;*
> *he remembers that we are dust.* (Ps. 103:13–14)

God knows our frame. He knows that we do not have a grasp of the big picture, except to the extent that we may believe what *He* has told us about it. But just a little bit later in this same psalm, God gives some staggering promises to what, in one respect, are just little bits of tumbleweed.

> *As for man, his days are like grass;*
> *he flourishes like a flower of the field;*
> *for the wind passes over it, and it is gone,*
> *and its place knows it no more.* (Ps. 103:15–16)

To judge from our experience, life is evanescent, transient, momentary, flickering. *Sic transit gloria mundi*—thus passes the glory of the world. The flashbulb popped, and life was over. Our lives are a vapor, James tells us. "What is your life? For you are a mist that appears for a little time and then vanishes" (James 4:14). Imagine driving down a stretch of country road early in the morning, with little wisps of fog coming off the creek bed that winds by the road. One of those wisps, no longer than your forearm, blows by your car and is gone. There goes a good metaphor for life.

In an agricultural society, the kind the psalmist lived in, an obvious image for this was that of the flowers of the field—green and verdant in the spring, but one good scorching wind and the beautiful flower game was over. Once this settles in on us, we are tempted to shrug our shoulders in despair and ask, "So what's the point?"

The point is that God is Lord of the whole river, and just because *we* don't know everything about it does not mean that He is as limited as we are. And He has promised us, provided we keep covenant with Him, some downstream blessings—after the scorching wind has turned everything out of its place. You see, five hundred years from now, the people living on the land where I currently live will know nothing whatsoever about me. My place will know me no more. Instead of despairing, I should realize that there is another way of keeping track. There is one who knows every detail of every story. Though my descendants in that day may not know me, and may have to use their generation's (much higher tech) version of Ancestry.com even to find out what my name was, I am still their father. And though I cannot know their names, there is One who knows all their names and birthdays, along with the number of freckles on each nose, and the same for all *their* great-grandchildren. And this is not just raw knowledge—it is knowledge that is prepared with a blessing in mind. This comes out in the next verses.

> *But the steadfast love of the Lord is from everlasting to*
> *everlasting on those who fear him,*
> *and his righteousness to children's children,*
> *to those who keep his covenant*
> *and remember to do his commandments.*
> *The Lord has established his throne in the heavens,*
> *and his kingdom rules over all.* (Ps. 103:17–19)

We are sometimes rattled by the greatness of God's promises to us, and so we come up with questions that mean that maybe this isn't quite what it seems. Oh, we say, that verse is in the *Old* Testament. They used to care about their subsequent generations a lot more back then.

The trouble with this kind of thinking is that our Lord's mother quoted this psalm, and not because the child in her womb was the one who was going to end all that kind of thing. No, the coming of the Christ is the time when these promises start seriously to be fulfilled. It was not the time when they were finally abrogated. And secondly, a brief glance at the generations of the Old Testament should tell us that that was not the time when God's promises of this sort were at all fulfilled.

That is when the promises were *given,* certainly, but Jeremiah could perhaps be excused for looking around and wondering what was happening in his day. But then he looked ahead to the time of the New Covenant and was greatly encouraged—God's goodness to the *offspring* of His people would last as long as the sun, moon, and stars would last (Jer. 31:35–36).

These blessings are not automatic. They are offered by grace and appropriated by faith. That faith is faith in God in the present, which is, incidentally, the only time we can believe. When we believe God for our fathers and our children, we are not making an idol out of family or family generations. We are believing God *for* our children; we are not believing *in* our children. The Lord Jesus said that we had to put Him first, and no question about it. "Whoever loves father or mother more than me is not worthy of me, and whoever loves son or daughter more than me is not worthy of me" (Matt. 10:37; cf. Luke 14:26). But when we seek first the kingdom in this way, we find that all these things are added to us again (Matt. 6:33; Luke 12:31). This includes family. Put family first, and you lose everything, including family. Put Christ first, and everything is restored to you—including houses, brothers and sisters, mothers, children, and lands (Mark 10:30). I take it that

He does not include fathers in that list because He is *speaking* to the fathers.

So we do not take whatever our fathers did as the standard. If they were faithful, we follow gladly in their faith. If they were not, then we must repent of their sins. But in either case, we own them as our fathers. This is the message of Psalm 78. In this psalm Asaph says that he will utter the dark parables and sayings that he learned from his fathers (v. 3). He will not hide these things from their children but will instruct the coming generation (v. 4). God established a law in Judah that required fathers to teach their children, who would teach *their* children . . . to do what? Two things are worth mentioning. The first was to hope in God, remembering His works, and another one was *to not be like their fathers* (v. 8). Faithful children follow a good example and refuse to follow a bad one. If our fathers' precepts were wiser than their actions, then we should honor them by refusing to duplicate their actions. "And I said to their children in the wilderness, Do not walk in the statutes of your fathers, nor keep their rules, nor defile yourselves with their idols" (Ezek. 20:18).

The love of God (to dried-up field flowers, remember) is a steadfast love. His love is from everlasting to everlasting, which pretty much seems to cover everything that needs to be covered. This love is for those who fear Him. His righteousness is to the grandchildren, and this is a self-perpetuating kind of thing. If the promise is good for the grandfather, it is good for the grandchild, who will one day be a grandfather himself. Those who keep covenant with Him, and who remember to do His commandments (the central one being to *believe*), will see generational blessings that will stagger the imagination.

Imagine, in the resurrection, being sought out by your descendants so that you can echo the words of Isaiah and the Lord Jesus, "Here am I, and the children you have given me" (see Isa. 8:18; Heb. 2:13).

But in order for this to happen, we have to remember one of the first things we noted in this book—fathers, if they are to be like God the Father, have to be present in the lives of their children. Failure at this point is one of the saddest features of the modern family.

Questions to Consider:

1. What are the two things that fathers are for?
2. What is the basis for saying this?
3. In what sense should men and women be treated as equals? In what sense not?
4. Why does history seem like a series of ponds to us? Why is it more like a river?
5. What are some of the passages of Scripture in which God promises us faithful descendants?

Chapter 3

A Culture of Absenteeism

Fatherless Times

Father hunger is one of the central maladies of our time, and when there is widespread hunger like this, it is obviously a manifestation of a shortage. Fathers are absent, or gone a lot, or they have somehow turned themselves away. Fortunately, the malady we have is treatable, but not as long as we remain in denial about it. The malady can be addressed, but we have to take care. There are some responses that can seem quite reasonable, but they don't take the larger biblical context into account. David Blankenhorn writes,

> The United States is becoming an increasingly fatherless society. A generation ago, an American child could reasonably expect to grow up with his or her father. Today, an American child can reasonably expect not to. Fatherlessness is now approaching a rough parity with fatherhood as a defining feature of American childhood.[1]

We live in fatherless times. We have the obvious problem of fatherlessness when the fathers are long gone, but we also have the problem of fatherlessness when the fathers are present but not accounted for. If fathers are on the premises but don't know what is expected of them, we have another kind of fatherlessness.

The symptoms of our fatherlessness are marked, and they are everywhere. In some ways, we have adjusted to it; and in others, we in the conservative Christian world have overreacted to this vacuum by trying to manufacture our own solutions to the problem, which invariably make it worse. Instead of this, we need to wait on the Lord, and also to ask Him to teach us what we are waiting for.

> Behold, I will send you Elijah the prophet before the great and awesome day of the LORD comes. And he will turn the hearts of fathers to their children and the hearts of children to their fathers, lest I come and strike the land with a decree of utter destruction. (Mal. 4:5–6)

When John the Baptist was asked directly if he was Elijah, he said that he was not (John 1:21). The question was a reasonable one. He was a prophet, *like* Elijah, and he dressed in the same way that Elijah did (2 Kings 1:8; Matt. 3:4). And yet, Jesus, when He was asked this same question, replied that John the Baptist was Elijah (Matt. 11:14; 17:10–12; Mark 9:11–13). The question was asked because of this prophecy—when Elijah came, it would be just prior to the great and dreadful day of the Lord. In other words, Malachi says that Elijah would come as a forerunner to the Messiah, which is precisely the role assigned to John the Baptist in the New Testament. What would the role of this Elijah be? His task would be to turn the hearts of the fathers to the children, and the hearts of the children to the fathers, lest God come and smite the earth with a curse.

We should note that the first commandment with a promise is the commandment to honor father and mother (Eph. 6:1–4). That promise was a promise of blessing for the land that God was giving. The first giving of the command was to the children of Israel at the foot of Sinai, and the land in question was the land of Canaan. But Paul reiterates this promise in a way that applies it to the Christian children of Ephesus, and the promise is not abrogated—rather, it is picked up and expanded to cover the entire earth. The relationship between parents and children is directly connected to a blessing on the land. Moreover, the contrary is also true. When there is a fundamental estrangement between fathers and children, the result of that unhappy mess will be that God will come and strike the land with a curse. In short, when fathers are blessed, the land is blessed. When fathers are cursed, the land is cursed.

It is interesting that the New Testament explicitly connects John to this prophecy, but it does not explicitly talk about this particular consequence of John's ministry. However, we know that this is what happened. So how did John bring this about? What did he preach? His was a baptism of repentance. His message was a message of *repentance*. "In those days John the Baptist came preaching in the wilderness of Judea, 'Repent, for the kingdom of heaven is at hand'" (Matt. 3:1–2).

His message was a corporate message for all of Israel. He was not only the forerunner of the Messiah, but he was exercising this office by declaring the approach of a *kingdom*. He was declaring this to the nation of Israel. The prophecy of Malachi said that the alternative to hearing Elijah's message would be that the earth would be struck with a curse. The relevant command of God (the fifth commandment) says that it is a command with a promise, that your days may be long in the land that the Lord your God is giving you (Deut. 5:16). As already noted, the New Testament citation of this expands the promise—that "you may live long in the land"

(Eph. 6:2–3). All of which is to say that this is not just another book on "the family." Larger issues are in play, and ultimately we are talking about the reformation of a mere Christendom.

Our temptation is to take passages like this one and give them a radical and individualized meaning. If you *personally* love Jesus, then you personally will have your children's hearts turned toward you, and you will be turned toward your children. This great eschatological announcement from Malachi, this prophecy of the turning point of all human history, turns out to be all about our white-bread family values and us. This is entirely inadequate, and we will see that the Scriptures are actually explicit on this point. Of course, families must be put right. But they cannot be put right without a number of other things being put right as well.

You cannot make an omelet without breaking a few eggs, as has been said. But as another fellow observed, it is amazing how many eggs you can break without ever making a decent omelet. Keep this in mind as we consider the following: "But seek first the kingdom of God and his righteousness, and all these things will be added to you" (Matt. 6:33). Jesus is here talking about food and clothing (both being family issues), but does He ever talk about the family directly? Well, yes. "If anyone comes to me and does not hate his own father and mother and wife and children and brothers and sisters, yes, and even his own life, he cannot be my disciple" (Luke 14:26).

Remember that John said to repent because a *kingdom* was about to arrive. And what will be the result of John's ministry? The hearts of the fathers will be turned, remember? So how do we harmonize this with the radical demands of Jesus that we have just been considering? That which is surrendered in death before God is always raised to life in God. This is true everywhere, in all areas of life, but is *especially* true of the family. It is mentioned by Malachi as one of the principal fruits of John's ministry.

Remember the eggs and omelets? If a man is an idolater—which means that his citizenship is primarily in some earthly kingdom—then he is not seeking first the kingdom of God. He has not heard John's words about an arriving *kingdom*. But he is not being told to repent of behavior that is personally destructive because "he needs to get his life together." He *does* need to get his life together, but not because Jesus is a twelve-step program. We are told to repent because His kingdom is near. If a man lives his life without reference to that kingdom, regardless of how conservative and traditional his family values might be, he is only breaking eggs and not making omelets. God is the One who establishes our corporate citizenship, and He has told us how to enter into it.

Malachi described the consequences of John's ministry, and this description was obviously the work of the Spirit of God. The hearts of the fathers will be turned to the children. The hearts of the children will be turned to the fathers. But we do not try to build strong families in order to build a strong kingdom for God. Rather, He has established an invincible kingdom, and when we seek this kingdom first, all these other things are added to us.

The fact that these other things have not been added to us, the fact that we live in fatherless times, reveals our attitudes toward God the Father. Father hunger is one of the chief symptoms of our idolatry. It is the basis for our political follies, our cultural follies, our technological follies, and so on. But the solution is not to schedule numerous family retreats. The solution is to announce, preach, and declare that the kingdoms of this world have become the kingdom of God, and of His Christ.

Another way of saying this is that men must seek to be Christians first. If they love Jesus Christ more than mother or father, or wife, or sons or daughters, then they will be in fellowship with the source of all love. If they make an idol out of any one of their family members, then they are out of fellowship with the source of all love—meaning that the "idol" is shortchanged. A man's wife receives far more love when she is number two after God than she would if she were number one. A man's children will be fathered diligently when they are loved in the context of a much greater love.

When a man seeks first the kingdom of God, among all the things that are added to him, we can expect to find the gift of authority numbered among them. When we love God, He gives us all we need in order to continue loving Him. If a man wants to love God, then one of the things he needs is the gift of true authority. Without that true authority, there is nothing that can be done to prevent a culture of paternal absenteeism from developing. That absenteeism will take the form of either fathers who *leave* or fathers who *detach*.

So how are we to understand authority? When Matthew tells us that Jesus taught with authority, and not like the scribes (Matt. 7:29), he is highlighting one of the perennial problems found in all forms of social organization. It is the problem found when someone who holds authoritative office does not have the charismatic authority to make it go. Such a man has one kind of institutional authority, and not another kind of personal authority. There is nothing wrong with institutional authority, but it is not meant to function on its own.

Two Kinds of Authority

These are, therefore, the two kinds of authority. One is the authority of office, which can be obtained in all sorts of ways. The other kind of authority is the kind that flows to the person who takes responsibility. This is a spiritual authority—the kind of authority that flowers when there has been death and resurrection.

Every father has the authority that comes with the office. This is why Scripture tells us to honor father and mother and does not put a series of special conditions on it. It does not say that we should honor our father, *provided* that he deserves it. The authority of office is an authority that Scripture recognizes and supports, even when the office-holder is clearly not up to the task. When Miriam and Aaron challenged Moses over the Ethiopian woman he had married, the result of the challenge was that Miriam was struck with leprosy. Moses cried out to the Lord for her healing, and the Lord responded with a statement that is quite interesting: "But the LORD said to Moses, 'If her father had but spit in her face, should she not be shamed seven days? Let her be shut outside the camp seven days, and after that she may be brought in again'" (Num. 12:14). It does not take a degree in family counseling to know that if a father spits in his daughter's face, all is not well in that household. In addition, it is equally clear that the *father* had let things get away from him, and he could have used some good books on child-rearing about fifteen years before this. And yet, at the same time, it is the daughter who is shamed and taken out of the camp, not the father. So the authority of office is one that we recognize and honor, even while noting that it is not sufficient.

The authority of office is like having the right checkbook with you. That is your name in the upper left-hand corner. It is your address, your account number. You are the authorized signatory on the account. The other kind of authority is like having money in the bank. If a man is bouncing checks left and right, it will do no good for him to complain that he still has checks left. I have seen many fathers who tried to write a big check that their children would clear for them, and they demanded that their children do this because they could prove (from the Bible) that it was their checkbook. I have been in counseling sessions trying to explain to a hapless father that his account had insufficient funds, with him trying to explain to me that he had read one of my books that taught that he, the father, was the owner of the checkbook. Both these assertions are quite true, but they are assertions about two completely different things.

In order to deal with the plague of fatherlessness, we have to return first to the worship of God the *Father*. But we can't have the Father without the Son, and we can't have the Son without the Spirit. Not only so, but we can't have any of them without the preaching of the gospel. The culture of absenteeism that we see around us is a function of how we worship. Theologian Henry Van Til taught us that culture is religion externalized. At the center of every culture is a *cultus*, a practice or principle of worship. In a Christian context, think of it as church and kingdom, church and parish. At the center of the community you have the house of worship. Outside that place of formal worship you have all the activities that men and women pursue. They ought to pursue in obedience to Christ, of course, but they ought not to pursue in the context of formal worship.

There are many lawful activities and pursuits that ought to be *excluded* from the sanctuary, even though they are taught, shaped, and informed *by* the ministry of the sanctuary. Examples would include lovemaking and auto mechanics, great naval battles and heart surgery. But in order to have these kingdom activities conducted rightly, it is necessary to have the worship at the center being conducted rightly. Worship is the necessary governor. This means that if we see a dearth of fathers in the realm outside worship, we must not try to organize pro-fatherhood rallies in that same realm. It will not work. The need of the hour is to return to the worship of God the Father, in the power of the Holy Spirit, and all conducted in the name of the Lord Jesus.

Trying to fix society without addressing the central issues of worship is futile in the extreme. A comparable exercise would be somebody who tried to establish a new hive of bees without organizing the new colony around a queen bee. It is not possible to go out into a fresh meadow and organize the bees there by waving your arms. The queen is essential. In the same way, worship is an essential principle in establishing any human culture. Everything else is just waving your arms in a meadow.

Of course, we are not endorsing everything that falls under the heading of "worship." Idolatrous worship will shape idolatrous cultures, and the worship of the true and triune God will result in true, human culture. Worship of the right God on paper will result in paper-thin Christian cultures—the kind that cannot withstand the assaults of unbelief.

This is how it works. In the Lord's Prayer, Jesus taught us to pray, and in the petition about the Father's kingdom, we learn something that is quite striking: "Your kingdom come, your will be done, on earth as it is in heaven" (Matt. 6:10). It would be very easy to connect this petition with nothing more than the cheerful alacrity of the angels. In other words, when God asks for something to be done in Heaven, the angels don't go around with pouty expressions, slamming doors behind them. Neither should we, or so this understanding of this petition goes. While this is all quite true (we shouldn't obey God with a surly attitude), there appears to be more going on here.

Jesus first tells us to pray that the Father's kingdom would *come*, not that it would *go*. We are praying the Father's will would be done on earth the same way it is done in Heaven. But we are saying this in a petition addressed to the Father in prayer. When we worship God the Father, the Bible teaches that we are ascending into the heavenly places in order to do so. This means that when we glorify God the Father in Heaven (in our worship), it is fully appropriate to ask God to then glorify His name on earth as it has just been glorified in Heaven. In doing so, we are asking Him to take the instrument of the worship we have offered and use it to glorify His name on earth—for it has been glorified in Heaven. The process of this happening is the process of God's kingdom coming to earth. This happens as we worship the *Father,* hallowing *His* name. It should go without saying that we do not hallow His name by being embarrassed by His name, or changing it to something that will not cause consternation in our local lesbian circles.

But if worship is the engine, and it is, and we want to move down the road, at some point we have to let the clutch out. If we recover an understanding of the Fatherhood of God (which can only be done if we worship in the name of His Son), then we will suddenly find ourselves seeing the malady of fatherlessness everywhere we look. If we want to connect the realities of worship to the needs of our culture, we will have to look at it with a true and evangelical faith. What is it that overcomes the world? Is it not our *faith* (1 John 5:4)?

Because we have worshipped the Father, we must then teach our boys. Most boys growing up need to be taught their strength, as when they are horsing around with their younger siblings. They are bigger, stronger, and much more influential, let us say, than they think they are. But the need for teaching this lesson doesn't disappear when boys get past the horsing-around stage. In their families, men are much more important, crucial, and influential *than they believe themselves to be*. It is the easiest thing in the world for a man to grow up, get married, have kids, and still think of himself the way he did when he was a boy. In the words of Mark Driscoll, he is "a boy who shaves." He believes that he is just one more person living in this household—just one more of the roommates. But our perceptions are not authoritative, especially our perceptions of ourselves.

The Bible tells us that fatherhood is the font of the triune Godhead, and that all fatherhood here on earth is a reflection of that deep and ultimate Fatherhood (Eph. 3:14–15). Jonathan Edwards says this:

> The Father is the Deity subsisting in the prime, unoriginated and most absolute manner, or the Deity in its direct existence. The Son is the Deity generated by God's understanding, or having an idea of himself, and subsisting in that idea. The Holy Ghost is the Deity subsisting in act, or the divine essence flowing out and breathed forth, in God's infinite love to and delight in himself.[2]

And again:

> It seems to me most probable that God has his infinite happiness but one way, and that the infinite joy he has in his own idea and that which he has in his Son is but one and the same.[3]

These words are heady, but they are also inspiring and invigorating. This means that, for good or ill, on our level, what a father does is *potent*. The Father stoops an infinite distance and requires us to call ourselves by the same name that He bears in infinite glory. It reminds me of the place in *The Lion, the Witch and the Wardrobe* when Aslan brings the statues back to life, including a lion, and then later refers to "us lions."

> The most pleased of the lot was the other lion, who kept running about everywhere pretending to be very busy but really in order to say to everyone he met, "Did you hear what he said? *Us lions.* That means him and me. *Us lions.* That's what I like about Aslan. No side, no stand-off-ishness. *Us lions.* That meant him and me." At least he went on saying this till Aslan had loaded him up with three dwarfs, one Dryad, two rabbits, and a hedgehog. That steadied him a bit.[4]

God the Father calls us fathers as well, but then He steadies us up a bit with a challenging job, a wife, four kids, a quarter of an acre with some tough spots for mowing, and a mortgage.

Words of reassurance, offered or withheld, are monumental in a child's growth. Words of encouragement, or exhortation, or patient teaching, are the same. When a child has grown up under the devastation of unremitting harshness (and sometimes not so unwitting), or the devastation of neglect, the one thing a father may not say is that it "was not that big a deal." Of course it was a big deal. The child is (hopefully) going to be praying the Lord's Prayer for the rest of his life. What will naturally, readily, come to mind whenever he starts, whenever he says, "Our *Father* . . ."? What does that *mean* to him in his bones, and who taught it to him?

Many years ago I was teaching a class of high school kids at a Christian school, during the time when *awesome* was the descriptor of pretty much everything. For some reason, I was at war with that general usage. I would tell the class that "the Grand Canyon is awesome, crab nebulae are awesome, and God is awesome. Your quiz scores are *not* awesome." I recall telling one bright young student there that I knew I could not make them stop saying that word. But I went on to say that I *could* behave in such a way that, throughout the rest of their lives, whenever they said it, they would cringe and think of me.

It is the same kind of thing with fathers. Fathers (whether they recognize it or not) are behaving in a way that will shape their children's understanding of what it means to be a father, and that understanding will occupy a central place in their lives. Are you their protector, or the principal thing they need protection *from*? Are you the provider, or the main impediment to provision? Are you the driving engine of joy in your household? Or the central reason for depression and sorrow? "But the main threat against which a man must protect his wife is *his own sin*."[5] The same thing goes for everyone else living in that home. He must protect them all, not only from outside threats, but also from a delinquent protector—himself.

I was speaking to an earnest father recently at a conference, and his dilemma was a very real one. He had grown up without a father, and in the providence of God, he was now married and had four boys. His question was straightforward: "How can I be a model when I have had no model?"

We are built to learn by imitation. The loss, when we have had nothing to imitate, is a real loss. At the same time, God has arranged things such that we can recover something of that loss by coming to know the Father. We do this by the means appointed. We are not the first fatherless generation in history, and we are not likely to be the last. The good news is good news to the fatherless. Just as we have a tendency to track our "father issues" into the sanctuary, the traffic does go both ways. God restores when we worship Him, and He restores us in this area. If we have come to Christ, we have to realize that Christ is in the Father. What does this mean, if we are in Him? "In that day you will know that I am in my Father, and you in me, and I in you" (John 14:20). In the gospel, the fatherless *no longer are.*

The foundational issue has been addressed, but there are still some remaining practical questions. God the Father may have restored us on the central issue, but a man might still not know how to teach his son to throw a ball, or how to read his Bible, or how to change the oil in his car. For that sort of thing, it would hardly address the issue to double down on the worship—if your church has two services, for example.

One of the things men can do is read didactic books (like this one), but there is something else I would recommend. Paul says that when Timothy came to the Corinthians, he would remind them of Paul's way of life (1 Cor. 4:17). We are able to imitate what we see, certainly, but we are also able to imitate what we hear about and what we read. Throughout the book of Acts, Luke reminds us of Paul's way of life as well, and does so through the written word. But this principle can be extended. I would recommend that men who have had a real shortage of practical examples should read biographies of *fathers*. This would include fathers of great men, fathers in the church, fathers on the mission field, fathers over navies, and fathers of countries.

Questions to Consider:

1. In Malachi 4:5–6, what messianic promise is given concerning father/children relationships?
2. Why is it so important to love Christ more than your family? Does this mean that your family will be shortchanged?
3. Describe the two kinds of authority that fathers may have.
4. What is the checkbook analogy for paternal authority?
5. How can men who had no model of fatherhood growing up be a model to their children?

Chapter 4

Masculinity, False and True

Cultural Authority

In the American military, a salute is rendered in a particular way—palm down. In the British military, the salute is offered differently—palm out. And yet they are both expressions of honor, meaning the same thing. What is the "essence" of a salute? Is it not the expression of honor? And is it not obvious that the "accidents" of a salute can vary by custom or culture? Sure thing—that seems clear enough. But it does not follow from this that honor is therefore invisible. Honor that is kept hidden in the heart (down where the "essentials" are) is not honor at all, but dishonor.

If a lowly servant in a palace is tipped back in his chair, feet on a nearby window sill, when the king comes in, we may grant that in different cultures the servant will do different things. He will jump to his feet in one kingdom, or take a knee in another. But what he will not do is stay right where he is, making sure to honor the king "in his heart."

Spiritual realities *start* in the heart. But if they never make it out, then they are stillborn. Honor limited to the heart is not honor, but dishonor. Love that is never expressed is not love unsullied by contact with the world, but rather a lack of love. I am fond of saying theology comes out your fingertips, and whatever it is that comes out your fingertips is your theology. In the biblical perspective, we are taught to get things right in the heart first so that we can get things right outwardly. "Woe to you, scribes and Pharisees, hypocrites! For you clean the outside of the cup and the plate, but inside they are full of greed and self-indulgence. You blind Pharisee! First clean the inside of the cup and the plate, that the outside also may be clean" (Matt. 23:25–26). The word rendered *that* in the last sentence is *hina,* "in order that." Clean the inside, Jesus says, *so that* the outside may be clean also.

This means we should get masculinity straight in the heart so that the badges of masculinity (which every culture necessarily has) can be understood in a straight manner as well. Sex roles, and sex badges, are *often* a matter of cultural definition. A kilt is not a dress, as everybody knows. Some might even say these signs are arbitrary. But we must also remember that cultures have the *authority* to assign these roles, just as a military service has the authority to define what constitutes a salute. And if the culture has this rightful authority, then members of that culture have the responsibility to submit to the definitions and not kick against them. A military unit embroiled in a debate over whether or not "this kind of salute" is an arbitrary imposition from a tyrannical authority is a military unit that has *already* lost its way.

The Bible never says that a "real man" must go hunting, or play football at some time in his life, or change the oil in his truck, or spend some time every weekend at Home Depot buying fix-it items. If someone were to define such activities—suitably arranged in a checklist—as the *essence* of true masculinity, then we would be justified to laugh him right out of the room. Such a person would argue that Lord Nelson wasn't a true naval hero because he never learned to salute the right way. And Caesar never changed the oil in his chariot either.

Nevertheless, in any given culture certain masculine roles will necessarily be *assigned*, and those boys and men who are embracing their masculinity rightly will gladly assume those roles. It is also the case that cultures never require men to do everything on the list—it is quite sufficient to pick up seven out of ten. But if we isolate any particular thing on the list, it would be the work of mere minutes to show how arbitrary this task or role is. Sure, but that doesn't mean it isn't essential. Do we abandon the use of any nouns until it can be shown that the sound involved wasn't "arbitrarily" selected?

No—words, dress, roles, manners, and the like are all means of communication. If we refuse to communicate (because all the means of communication at our disposal are full of arbitrary ingredients), then we are going to go through life as mimes . . . until it occurs to us that even *that* is just more of the same.

In our day, we have attempted to deny all this. George Gilder points to the foolishness of the current consensus: "The principal tenets of sexual liberation or sexual liberalism—the obsolescence of masculinity and femininity, or sex roles, and of heterosexual monogamy as the moral norm—have diffused through the system and become part of America's conventional wisdom."[1] In simple terms, it has become *normal* to laugh at differing cultural roles for the two sexes.

We lost the heart of masculinity, and all we had left over were the residual badges from the last cultural era that assigned them. As time went on, it became easier and easier to make fun of the badges as entirely capricious. Why should men take out the garbage? Ho, ho, ho . . . Why can't women open their own car doors? But when a man opens the car door for his wife, *he is doing far more than just getting the door open.* It is not a matter of utility. It is not a question of pragmatics. Granted, we could save energy all around if both individuals opened their own doors. But he is making a statement in addition to getting the door open. He is disciplining his own heart and soul, which need it, and he is honoring his wife, who is glorified by it. The role of the man here, if we may speak this way, is not just to get the door open. His central role is the liturgical act of saying that women everywhere should be held in honor by men, and that he adds his *amen* to this, as everyone in the parking lot at Costco can now see.

If we are faithful in a little, we will be found faithful over much (Luke 16:10). If we are muddled in the little things, we will be muddled in matters of great import. This is why the whole question of women serving in combat has been covered over with multiple layers of lies. The modern American military has become quite a conflicted place—demanding courage of its members in action while simultaneously demanding that these same people be craven cowards when it comes to their own careers. It is required of them that they deny the obvious in order to remain eligible for promotion.[2] Women were not built for fighting, but neither are the military men who are too cowardly to point out that obvious fact.

By playing these games about "arbitrary" gender roles, we have not succeeded in outlawing masculinity, but we have robbed it of much of its vocabulary. There are not very many acceptable ways to speak "masculine" anymore. We are all in denial, and the results are not pretty. Gilder again:

> [M]asculinity is treated like sex in Victorian England: a fact of life that society largely condemns and tries to suppress and that its intellectuals deny. . . . The result is a society that at once denies the existence of natural male aggressiveness and is utterly preoccupied with it.[3]

While the vocabulary of masculinity can vary from culture to culture, the underlying reality does not. We are dealing with a fact as nonnegotiable as gravity and as practical as potatoes. This means that women are not victims of oppression because they have taken up certain roles; they have sought out the roles that they have wanted, just as the men have. Only those in the grip of an ideology are prepared to dispute it.[4]

Fathers need to be masculine, and they need culturally assigned ways to express it profitably. In order to be biological fathers, men simply need to be male, but to be real *fathers,* they need to be masculine. Moreover, they need to be seen as being masculine. But before we press that point too much, perhaps we should spend some time defining what it means.[5] And that means some debris clearing first—masculinity has some counterfeits out there.

Recalling what we have already covered about the need for culturally assigned sex roles, masculinity does not mean talking out the side of your mouth.[6] It doesn't mean swagger, or machismo, or a swaggering machismo. It does not mean bluster or bravado, or wearing wife-beaters. It does not mean brittle egos or cinder blocks for brains.[7] It does not mean quoting the apostle Peter woodenly, to the effect that the little woman ought to be calling him "lord" more than she does. Even if she did, the effect might not be what he wants. "Sometimes the word *lordship* can rankle us," says Richard Phillips. "We easily associate the word . . . with images of overfed men in castles wearing powdered wigs and strange clothing."[8]

On the opposite side, neither does it mean getting in touch with your inner little girl. It does not simper and lisp. Masculinity is not metrosexual.[9]

So what *is* masculinity? We'll get there in a minute, but another thing to shake is the equation of masculinity with simple maleness. Feminism has spent quite a bit of energy trying to equate the two, a mistake helped along by the way God the Father was represented on the ceiling of the Sistine Chapel, but this is really quite simplistic. Christian theology holds that God the Father is a *Spirit* (John 4:24), and one of the characteristics of spirits is that they don't have biological anything, and this would mean (it would seem to follow) that they don't have biological sex. We don't ask, for example, whether archangels are cold-blooded or warm-blooded. The question doesn't really apply. Angels don't have blood.

The difference between God the Father and the angels is that He is an uncreated Spirit, but He is a Spirit nonetheless. This means that His masculinity is *not* a function of Him being male. God the Father is not male, but He is still ultimately masculine. C. S. Lewis makes a helpful observation by building on this point:

> "Since God is in fact not a biological being and has no sex, what can it matter whether we say He or She, Father or Mother, Son or Daughter?" But Christians think that God Himself has taught us how to speak of Him.[10]

This might seem like a trivial point, but actually a great deal rides upon it. The position that God is a biological male (as Zeus plainly was, contributing much to Hera's exasperation) is a view that theologians of another age would have called "a heresy." When we call Him *Father*, we are not saying (or implying) that He is male in any way. What we are saying is that He is ultimately masculine, and that every masculine office in the created order reflects that masculinity in some way, partaking in it somehow. The historic Christian position here is that God has taught us how to speak of Him because there was something we plainly *needed to learn*. We needed to learn it because we didn't know it yet.

So we do not call God *Father* because we have projected our notions of male-based fatherhood up into the heavens. We call Him Father because traces of His masculinity have been bestowed on us.

A father down here partakes of Fatherhood in some mysterious way. The apostle Paul tells us in Ephesians that "all fatherhood derives its name" from God the Father.

> For this reason I bow my knees before the Father, from whom every family in heaven and on earth is named, that according to the riches of his glory he may grant you to be strengthened with power through his Spirit in your inner being. (Eph. 3:14–16)

The phrase rendered here as "every family" is literally *pasa patria*—all fatherhood derives its name from our heavenly Father. This particular rendering of "all fatherhood" makes it explicit, but the point remains unchanged even if we go with the more general translation of "every family." Every family is named in accordance with "the Father," which means that fatherhood is essential to every family—even, maybe especially, in families where fathers are absent in any number of ways. Even feminists who try to take the step of refusing to take the last name of their husbands are still stuck with the indignity of keeping the last name of their *fathers*. Calling the attempts to undo all this by the name "feminism" is like calling the attempt to turn cats into dogs something like "felinism."[11] A family is named a *patria*. So a family is more than just roommates, or a legally recognized living arrangement, and home is more than where you hang your hat.

The entire created order declares and exhibits the glory of God. The heavens declare His handiwork (Ps. 19:1–6), and the whole creation displays His majesty, power, and might (Rom. 1:19–20). Everything reflects Him in some way; everything we see around us "answers to" something within the Godhead, somehow and some way. God has taught us that fathers and husbands are reflectors, in some way, of His masculinity. Men are not the source of this, but they are to be specified carriers of it.

Within our common realm of discourse, we speak of men as masculine and women as feminine. This is fully appropriate, and we will be following that common way of speaking throughout the course of this book—but it is only appropriate if we do it in a qualified way, if we do not absolutize it. We need to remember the qualifications made above. We know that we have absolutized this reality wrongly if we wind up thinking of God the Father as "the Old Man upstairs." We have absolutized it in a destructive way if we leave any room for the feminist misunderstanding and misrepresentation of God the Father *as male*. Our response to this should be that our males down here are only a dim, flickering image of what true masculinity is. We do not project our ideas of fatherhood up onto the big screen of the heavens. No, God's ultimate idea of fatherhood is projected down onto the little screens that each of us carries around. And the source of all this is far larger than any of us can possibly conceive.

Of course, if everything in creation reflects some aspect of God's glory, this would include women as well. Men and women *together* bear the image of God. "So God created man in his own image, in the image of God he created him; male and female he created them" (Gen. 1:27). This means that women, too, are screens that reflect the glory of the Father. Because of our regnant follies, we have to take care to avoid giving the impression that God somehow "has a feminine side." But this does mean that women are not excluded from this general principle. After all, in the book of Proverbs, a *son* is told to obey the law of his *mother* (Prov. 1:8; 6:20). It is not as though every aspect of all creation displays something of the character and nature of God, except for women.

These are deep waters for us, and to return to the point made earlier by Lewis, this means we should talk about God the way He taught us to talk about Him. We call God *Father*, not as a bit of theological speculation on our part, but rather as a matter of creaturely submission. The disciples asked Jesus to *teach* them how to pray (Luke 11:1), and so He did. He said they should pray, saying,

"Our Father . . ." When Jesus taught us to pray in this way, it is fair to assume that there is something here for us to *learn.*

It is too often glibly said that when Scripture teaches us to speak about the Father in this way, it was simply doing so in accommodation to the patriarchal times back then. Modern ideas about women participating in divine things would have been outrageous to them, and so it is not surprising that the biblical writers sought to avoid giving offense to that benighted and patriarchal world. Like many popular objections to biblical truth, this response is 180 degrees out from the way it actually was. The ancient world had no problems whatever with priestesses in religious service, and no problems at all with recognizing goddesses and consorts for the gods. The striking thing about the biblical faith is that this element, so *common* in the ancient world, is entirely missing. The biblical faith, with its highlighted masculinity, stands out in sharp relief against the ancient systems of unbelief—in much the same way that it stands out against modern systems of that same sort of unbelief.

What Masculinity Is

So what is it then? What is masculinity? Simply put, masculinity is the glad assumption of sacrificial responsibility. A man who assumes responsibility is learning masculinity, and a culture that encourages men to take responsibility is a culture that is a friend to masculinity.[12] When a culture outlaws masculinity, they soon learn that such outlaws are a terrible bane to them, instruments that destroy civilization with their mutant forms of masculinity. Every society needs masculine toughness, but it needs a toughness that lives and thrives and is honored within the boundaries of the law. And if we want this kind of toughness in the men, we have to teach it to the boys and cultivate it in them. Like a concrete foundation, masculine toughness has to lie underneath masculine tenderness.[13]

Masculinity is authoritative, and the Scriptures teach that authority flows to those who take responsibility, and it flees from those who seek to evade it. But we need to keep qualifying this because, in our attempts to get around what God has told us to do, we have distorted the definitions of many of these words—*authority* and *responsibility*, for starters. So authority flows to those who take responsibility through *sacrificial* service, just as Jesus did.

The Bible calls this assumption of responsibility headship, and we see that it extends far beyond the limits and boundaries of biological sex. "But I want you to understand that the head of every man is Christ, the head of a wife is her husband, and the head of Christ is God" (1 Cor. 11:3).

There is much to discuss here, but for the present I simply want to point out that the headship of God over Christ clearly does *not* mean that God is male and Christ female. And the fact that Christ is head over every man does not mean that Christ is male and every man is female. These categories of headship and submission do show up in the relations between husbands and wives, but they are clearly not bounded by or defined by sex. We have to fight off a bundle of mistaken assumptions, and this is why Scripture has to be our guide—and not the ambiguities found in "traditional values." Which tradition could that possibly be? Headship is tied to masculinity, but not automatically to maleness. When a male is a husband or father, he is summoned to the masculine role, and he has been equipped for it. This is certainly true, but the fact that all males are called to be masculine does not mean that all that is masculine is called to be male. All cows are mammals, but not all mammals are cows.

A related mistake that is readily made is assuming headship and authority are tied to bossing everybody around. In addition, we think that submission means we are arguing for a necessary inequality. But that is not what it means in Scripture at all. As we have just seen, the head of Christ is God. Paul tells us elsewhere that Christ did not consider His equality with God something to be grabbed at, but rather emptied Himself, taking the form of a servant (Phil. 2:5–9). For orthodox Christians who believe in the Trinity, "having a head" does not turn you into a zero. Jesus had a head, God the Father, and He is equal in His essence to God, who was nevertheless His head. He submitted to that head, being obedient to the point of death. So in the Christian lexicon, *submission does not mean inequality.* Just as headship does not mean male, submission to headship does not mean that women are relegated to the realm of chattel. Feminism is therefore, at its root, a Trinitarian heresy. God the Son is subordinate to God the Father, but subordination is not inequality of essence. Jesus Christ, the one who submitted and obeyed, was fully and completely God.

Christian men who are taught the ways of Christian masculinity are being taught to imitate Jesus Christ. But when Jesus taught us masculinity, He did this by submitting Himself to the point of death. Biblical authority knows how to bleed for others. So masculinity is the glad assumption of sacrificial responsibility, and this is what Jesus established for us. Christian husbands are commanded to love their wives in just that way—as Christ loved the church and gave Himself up for her. Christian husbands are explicitly commanded to imitate Christ at just this point (Eph. 5:25).

The foundation of all Christ's authority in the church is the blood that He shed. He took responsibility through sacrificial service, and therefore all authority flowed to Him. He shed His blood as He was assuming responsibility for the sins of all His people; therefore God has highly exalted Him. Jesus took the rap for things He didn't do—that's the model we are to live out.

When a culture goes to war with these truths, as ours has, it messes up the men far more than it does the women. This is because masculine roles need to be taught and taken up, as though they were crosses (because that is what they actually *are*), while feminine roles are more "built in."[14] A man's sexual identity is almost incidental to him. I am speaking obscurely, I know, but a young man has to go out and find his masculinity. He has to hunt around and discover it. When he does find it, he has to pick it up and carry it. If it is biblical masculinity, it is extremely heavy, and can only be carried by a miracle of divine grace. Masculinity is not something he can discover by looking at his own physiology, or at his yearning desire for sex and supper, most preferably for free. A woman's identity is wrapped up in her very being—she is a much more sexually attuned being than a man is. From her neck to her knees, she is in touch with her sexuality. She doesn't need to go find it—it is right there. Meantime, masculinity has to do with *performance*, whether on mountain peaks, on battlefields, or as a lover, which explains a lot of male anxieties.

Marriages are built on sex roles.[15] When boys are not trained in these sex roles, they come to think (because this is easy for males to think) that assuming responsibility consists of telling others what *their* responsibilities are. When masculinity is not taught and disciplined, boys grow up thinking that it means *selfishness* instead of *sacrifice*. Because it is a lot easier to pry men away from the sex roles assigned to them by their culture than it is to do with the women, this means it is easier to get selfish men than it is to get selfish women.

In the secular world, this idea of masculinity has been largely abandoned. In the conservative end of the Christian church, it has been quietly redefined. As a consequence, we are like those lost in the woods with what we thought were working compasses, not knowing that the magnetic pole has been taken away. Consequently, we are utterly disoriented. Getting back on the right path means we must return to a definition of masculinity that is the same as the way God defines it.

So in many ways we set boys up to fail as fathers. First, we do not teach them what the responsibilities of the masculine calling actually are. We leave them undirected and undisciplined. Second, when this undisciplined testosterone gets to be a problem, instead of dealing with it appropriately, the way a wise father would, we shunt them off into special programs, or have the school nurse hit them on the head with a chemical rock, or do our best to make sure they move toward the restraints of juvenile detention. And third, while they are in this beat-up condition, we teach them a false view of the relationship between the sexes. We tell them (in effect) that the only way to assert their masculinity is by means of engaging in the male act of penetration, and have thereby created a generation of lost and listless men. And with the ubiquity of porn, we are now looking to take even *that* away.

A man, when he takes on the responsibilities of being a husband and father, is shouldering the responsibilities of being masculine in that relationship, in that setting, in that calling. He is called to an authority that bleeds for others. He has a purpose for being here, and it is a purpose that God honors highly. So should we.

When we don't, all hell breaks loose. If you look out your window right now, that's it running down your street. It might even be running through your house. The next several chapters are concerned with what happens when we treat fathers as if they're expendable familial and societal add-ons.

Questions to Consider:

1. What happens when the "inside of the cup" is cleansed?
2. In what ways are culturally assigned sex roles constant and in what ways are they relative to each culture? What is the importance of communication in this?
3. When a man opens a car door for a woman, what else is happening?
4. Why do we call God our Father?
5. What definition of masculinity is given in this chapter?

Chapter 5

Atheism Starts at Home

Vanguard of the Fatherless

Whenever any sociological feature becomes pronounced in a society, that feature will of course have its advocates—its prophets and priests. I would argue that the new militant atheism that has appeared in our midst over the last decade can actually be understood as the intellectual vanguard of our fatherlessness. Fatherlessness, it turns out, has its apologists. These men are able to defend fatherlessness quite capably, for they were in fact shaped by it and want in turn to shape it further. They want to make more of what made them. But there is a perverse twist in this—father hunger made them, and so this means that what they want to usher in is a larger famine for others.

As I once had the privilege of engaging the late Christopher Hitchens in a series of debates on atheism, I noticed there were two topics that would predictably get quite a robust reaction out of him. One was the substitutionary atonement of Christ, and the other was any kind of declaration that God was an ever-present Father.

Hitchens saw this latter doctrine as oppressive, as suffocating. God was everywhere, looking over every shoulder and peering into every heart. This was for Hitchens nothing other than a nightmare cooked up by spiritual totalitarians—is the cosmos nothing more than a gigantic North Korea?

To understand where this sentiment came from, we have to go back a few centuries—taking a theological tour of Western civilization, and all within the scope of a few paragraphs. After the conversion of Constantine and the establishment of Christendom, the conception of God that dominated Western thought was that of the triune God of Scripture—and this for well over a thousand years. In the modern era, as our cultural apostasy began to pick up speed, the doctrine of the Trinity was abandoned for a "simpler," more streamlined view, which turned out to be various forms of Unitarianism, a theism much more conducive to the natural mind. God was still "there" and involved, but He was now a solitary monad in the sky.

Because of this, it was no longer possible to *identify* Him with love, as the apostle John had done (1 John 4:16). For in order for Him to *be* love, there must be a beloved within His Godhead. Prior to creation, if God was the ultimate hermit, the ultimate bachelor, there would be no beloved there to love. All you would have is a lonely, bachelor god and an empty pizza box. If it was not good for man to be alone (Gen. 2:18), it is unthinkable that God in His eternity would be alone. For orthodox Christians, the eternal reality of the Godhead has included, in its very nature, divine fellowship. The Father has always loved the Son, and the Son has loved the Father in return. Their Spirit is the eternal Spirit of that love, Himself an infinite third. With Unitarianism, at least initially, God was still interested in us, but it turns out there is no real grounded reason why He should have been. So one day He took off, and there we were, the foundling race. Ours was a planet full of children, ditched by Dad, just like a lot of American kids today. And that is how we got to your basic Deism.

After He had been gone awhile, it became easy to assert that He had never actually been around. So the older kids told the younger kids that it was all just a "dad myth," the kind of tale so often told in primitive tribes—or so clever scholars in anthropological studies tell us.[1] Ingenious explanations were offered to explain how it was that our family here just happened, and the little kids bought it.

So first there was the Father of Jesus Christ, Giver of the Holy Spirit. Then there was the Unitarian clockmaker God, who still watches His clock, and who was willing to do repairs from time to time. Then there was the god of the Deists, one who initially made the clock, wound it up, and then left, leaving no forwarding address. After He had been gone awhile, it was decided by general (very *scientific*) consensus that clocks can assemble themselves, and who needed a clockmaker anyway? This was the advent of modern atheism, a "scientific" and "rational" atheism. But after a few generations of that, we are now teetering on the edge of a postmodern atheism—one that denies any ultimate clockmaker the right to manufacture any metanarrative whatsoever. But ironically, this opens up space for the lesser deities, for the principalities and powers of the air, not to mention the things that go bump in the night. There's that ominous ticking sound, but it's not just clocks anymore.

In other words, we *drifted* away from God. Each stage of that drift was marked by a distortion of what He had revealed about Himself. Before we denied Him, we misrepresented Him. Before we said He was not there, we sidled away from Him, giving various excuses. In short, we didn't like Him very much at first, and it was after that we started saying He wasn't there at all. By the time Nietzsche declared God was dead, we had long since been acting as though He ought to have been dead. Nietzsche put it memorably:

> God is dead. God remains dead. And we have killed him. How shall we comfort ourselves, the murderers of all murderers? What was holiest and mightiest of all that the world has yet owned has bled to death under our knives: who will wipe this blood off us? What water is there for us to clean ourselves? What festivals of atonement, what sacred games shall we have to invent? Is not the greatness of this deed too great for us? Must we ourselves not become gods simply to appear worthy of it?[2]

Whatever this is, it is not disinterested scholarship discovering that it turns out after extensive research that God never existed. ("Oh *my*, look at this.") No, God has always existed as a *rival*. Denial of His existence is simply a weapon to use against such a rival. This is why Christopher Hitchens's use of the term *antitheist* is more apropos than the more common *atheist*. It may even be more fitting than the antitheists themselves recognize.

I have said a number of times before that there are two tenets to modern atheism. The first is that the atheist says there is no God, and the second is that the atheist hates Him. He hates Him for deserting us, for leaving us. At the same time, there is acknowledgment of the fact that we rejected God first. We demanded that He leave. We hate it when He leaves, and we hate it worse when He stays. This is all admittedly conflicted and contradictory, but one of the things we have to understand is that sin doesn't make sense. If it made some kind of sense, it wouldn't be sin. The world is not coherent if Christ is not there, and one of the things we have to stop doing is trying to help the atheist make sense of things even if Christ is not there. It doesn't. It won't. It can't.

Thomas Smail points out one side of this conflict:

> Unless the whole image of fatherhood is corrected or even redeemed, we shall almost inevitably project onto God the father

> we have loved or missed, have desired or resented, so that our adult spiritual life will be secretly controlled by our reactions to our early family life.[3]

Samuel Beckett puts it this way in his one-act play *Endgame*: "Let us pray to God . . . the bastard! He doesn't exist!" This is the side of atheism that hates or spitefully resents God the Father. C. S. Lewis remembers the way it was for him during his unhappy time as an atheist.

> I was at this time living, like so many Atheists or Antitheists, in a whirl of contradictions. I maintained that God did not exist. I was also very angry with God for not existing. I was equally angry with Him for creating a world.[4]

This is the anger of a deserted and petulant child. But of course, part of this package is the previous anger of the *un*deserted child—the one who resented the *presence* of the Father. In Paul Vitz's insightful treatment of the psychology of atheism, he remarks on this feature of it: "And of course the Oedipal dream is not only to kill the father and possess the mother or other women in the group, but also to displace the father. Modern atheism has attempted to accomplish this."[5]

Christopher Hitchens has repeatedly stated that the God of orthodox Christianity is "always there" and "won't get out of the way." An earthly father usually dies before his son does, leaving him his time on earth to be large and in charge. But if God the Father is immortal and never dies, then how can we ever replace Him? How can we get around Him, or past Him? With God the Father, this fundamental revolt in our hearts is an impossible dream. The serpent told us that we could be as God . . . he *promised*. In our fallenness, we want the setup to be more like Saturn overthrowing his father Uranus, and Zeus overthrowing his father Saturn. That's more like it. These are divine fathers who, if they won't move aside for you, can be *made* to move aside for you. But the triune God is the one who inhabits eternity and the only thing we can do about this inexorable revolt in our hearts against Him is to deny that He was ever there at all. But this is not a realization or reason; it is simply rebellion.

Of course, there is no systematic way to sort all this out. It is a perfect jumble. In order to unravel the contradictions, we must deal with the realities of *sin*. In other words, to whatever extent we have been deserted by God, we deserved every bit of it. To the extent that He has not left us alone, it is a staggering mercy, and not an officious meddling or interference. This reality is the photo negative of what the angry atheist feels—he believes that if we were deserted, it was entirely unjustified. And if God were to come back into our lives to make things right, He would bungle that reentry too, and would not let us stand on our own two feet. In other words, the atheist feels that God is always wrong, and that he, the atheist, could always do a better job of being god over his own life. And so that is what he sets out to be and do.

In the midst of considering these things, it once occurred to me that one of the breeding grounds for this modern atheism may well be the English boarding school system. Take your nation's best and brightest, take your most precocious sons, and send them away to boarding school. Give them a first-rate education, apart from mother and apart from dad. What could go wrong? Christopher Hitchens lost his faith at boarding school, as did his brother Peter (although Peter returned to the faith). C. S. Lewis lost his faith at boarding school. Atheist Richard Dawkins went to boarding school. There is a graduate thesis in there for somebody.

Fathers As a Theology Primer

The family is an analogy of the cosmos. God intends for children to learn about His Fatherhood *by this analogy first.* A two-year-old boy shaking the crib at 3:30 a.m. is not doing so because he is troubled by the vision cast in *Thus Spake Zarathustra.* He is not being vexed by theological or philosophical problems. But he *is* studying what fatherhood is like.

Fathers are speaking about God the Father constantly. They do not have the option of shutting up. What they are saying may be true or false, but they are not in a position where they can refuse to say anything. A father who just sits and stares, a father who is down at the office all the time, a father who deserts the family, a father who just donated sperm at the sperm bank—all of them are speaking. Every one of them is saying something all the time. A father who teaches his son to swing a bat, a father who listens to his daughter explain why Peter Rabbit shouldn't have disobeyed, a father who kisses their mom on the lips, a father who reads for hours to the family in the evening—all of them are speaking too.

But this is not said as though children are just empty receptacles, ready to mindlessly receive whatever the father puts in. No, earthly fathers need to understand that this atheism dynamic (because we are fallen) is also at play in their relationship with their children. There is a self-will that wants to reject parental authority and, in the words of every two-year-old, "*me* do it." There is also a childlike dependence that wants the father to overcome that disobedience, in order to prove that he loves the child enough to deal with as small an obstacle as this petty and childish rebellion. Children need to be fathered despite their resistance, and they want to be fathered, and the ratios between those two sentiments vary. A wise father studies those ratios and works with them.

This is why fathers need to learn how to be strict in the same way that God the Father is strict, and to be merciful in the same way that He is merciful. If we are strict only, we crush the spirit out of our children, or we provoke rebellion.[6] If we are merciful only, we create a culture of entitlement and self-indulgence in the home. And, in the worst possible combination, if we are strict where God is merciful, and merciful where God is strict, then we are busy supplying the strip clubs of the future with all their pole dancers and customers.

The atheist has certain caricatures of God, and clever atheists are quite adept at describing those caricatures in some detail. But one of the reasons they are good at this is that they have seen fathers who are living models of that caricature. There is a profound way to guard against that caricature, to inoculate your children against it, which we will consider in a moment. But before getting to that, we should consider what the atheist would say to a simple response that God is a *loving* God.

Suppose we reply that God is not like a totalitarian despot at all. The two things do not compare. We pray, "*Dear* heavenly Father . . ." But the atheist replies that all totalitarian states do the "Dear Leader" thing. We say that God provides for us. The atheist comes back with the observation that this is just what the overweening state does—cradle-to-grave security. We say that God hears all our prayers, even the faintest whisper. The atheist answers that Big Brother had a pretty effective surveillance system too. The only thing our religion doesn't share with totalitarianism would be the goose-stepping and the big missile parades.

But this overlooks one thing, and it is pretty significant. The similarities can all be granted, but there is a hidden premise that makes this unbelieving argument seem compelling. Once that premise is brought out into the open, the self-evident nature of the comparison starts to evaporate. Debunkers like to pretend that whenever you find two similar things, the purer one must be an imitation of the fouler one.[7]

This doctrine is more prevalent than we might think. We have gotten used to its presence, which is not the same thing as understanding the fallacy. A husband making love to his wife is doing "the same thing" that a rapist does to his victim—and feminists conclude that that fair one is a copy of the foul. Matrimony is therefore legitimized and subordinated rape.

It should be clear to us that the desire for the foul thing to be "real" and the fair thing a "knock off" is an emotional decision. How can a father guard his kids against this particular emotional drift, and how can he answer his atheist friend at work? The answer may be surprising—it is not a substitute for careful argument, but it provides a necessary backdrop for any such arguments to become visible. In fact, if we do all things without grumbling or moaning (Phil. 2:14–15), the apostle Paul tells us that we will stand out as shining lights against the backdrop of a crooked generation.

Paul also tells us what the two fundamental sticking points for unbelievers are. He says that those who do not know God are suppressing the truth in unrighteousness, and the two tenets that they suppress in particular are the fact that God is God, and the necessity of giving thanks to Him: "For although they knew God, they did not honor him as God or give thanks to him, but they became futile in their thinking, and their foolish hearts were darkened" (Rom. 1:21).

Note that they—despite knowing God—refused to honor Him as God, and they refused also to render thanks to Him. The two things, therefore, that atheism is trying to get away from should be the two things that Christians are bringing up and exhibiting themselves all the time. Christians should make sure that they themselves honor God as God, and that they overflow with thanksgiving. If the atheist wants to run from something, our task is to make sure that whatever that might be is right *there*, breathing on their neck.

The way we represent the Fatherhood of God, therefore, is by embracing and exulting in the sovereignty of God over all things, and by overflowing with gratitude to Him for all things. God works out *all* things in accordance with the good pleasure of His will (Eph. 1:11). We are called, always and everywhere, to give thanks for all things—"giving thanks always and for everything *to God the Father* in the name of our Lord Jesus Christ" (Eph. 5:20). The problem with this, as you no doubt will have heard from the atheist, is a little something called "the problem of evil." If God is sovereign over all things in the cosmos, the atheist has some criticisms he would like to file with the complaint department.

If God is all good and all powerful, then why is there evil here? It is for this alleged reason that the atheist refuses to honor God as God. And the existence of evil makes it impossible to offer up any prayers of thanksgiving. Therefore there is no Father. N. D. Wilson asks the question this way:

> But can this God, the God who made moths to worm my apples and birds to eat the worms; the God who allowed His characters to displease Him, to grieve Him; the God who allowed death and decay to enter stage left, who allows shadows in His paintings and damning flaws in His characters—can that God be good, let alone perfect?[8]

The first thing Christians need to do is to stop feeling bad about the atheist's statement of the problem of evil. As I wrote to Christopher Hitchens, it is far better to believe in God and acknowledge the problem of evil than to be an atheist and to have no way of even *defining* the evil that you have mysteriously come to believe constitutes such a problem. "I reply that I would rather have my God *and* the problem of evil than your no God and 'Evil? No problem!'"[9]

The second thing is to exult in the fact that God is the God in, over, and under all things. Whatever is happening in the world, it is not resulting in God wringing His hands over it and saying, "Oh *dear* . . ."

Siloam and the Problem of Evil

It is quite striking there are two places in the New Testament that discuss a place named Siloam in Jerusalem, and in both places people are misinterpreting instances of natural evil. In one place a tower at Siloam fell, killing eighteen (Luke 13:4–5). In the other place Jesus healed a man who had been born blind (John 9:1–11). The tower disaster had caused people to think that the victims must have been "above average" sinners in particular, and Jesus corrects this false impression. In John, Jesus says that the man was born blind so that God's works could be made manifest. Jesus anointed his eyes with spittle and dirt and then sent him to the pool of Siloam. John, who tells us that Siloam means "sent," makes it obvious that this was symbolic and significant. The blind man did what he was told and so his sight was restored.

So both passages involve the place Siloam. Both passages involve people misinterpreting the meaning of the misfortune of others. In one place they thought the eighteen were worse sinners than anybody. In the other they asked who had sinned, this man or his parents, that he had been born blind. In both places the word *Siloam* means the same thing—"sent."

As we consider these things, we should beware of reading the decrees of God glibly. We should not rush to assign meanings, or jump to facile conclusions. As Jesus said elsewhere: "Do not judge by appearances, but judge with right judgment" (John 7:24). At the same time, we know from Scripture that God is God over all things.

If disaster befalls a city, has not the Lord done it (Amos 3:6)? We know that God freely and unalterably ordains whatsoever comes to pass, and yet in such a manner as to not displace the freedom and responsibility of us as His image bearers. Further, we know what those decrees are, after the event (James 4:15). Once something has happened, we know *that* it happened in the good pleasure of God. But even though we know what has occurred, we only know a tiny fraction of what has occurred. Consequently, what we don't know yet (fully) is *why*. For help with that, we must be steeped in the scriptural take on the world, which will enable us to offer our understanding with a humble confidence and a confident humility. For the rest, we are willing in patience to postpone a fuller understanding. As the old gospel song has it, "Farther along, we'll know all about it, farther along, we'll understand why."

We can have this confidence because we have been made sons and daughters of the Father. We are not fatalists; we are not Stoics. We are not resigning ourselves to some inescapable fate of having gotten ourselves caught in the machinery. If we are reeling under the weight of natural disasters, or personal disasters, or a world groaning for the redemption of all things, we have to remember that a scriptural view of the world places the cross of Jesus Christ at the very crux of this world. The God who governs all things has revealed Himself in His Son—the God who bled. He said that when He was lifted up, He would draw all men to Himself. So our comfort is not in some Panglossian metaphysical argument. Our comfort is that the author of this great disaster story wrote Himself into the very center of that disaster, that He might carry the weight of it Himself. Surely this suggests a deeper meaning than the simplistic one offered by Job's false comforters?

If we rest in God's sovereignty *alone*, we will become fatalistic determinists. If we rest in Christ's sufferings alone, detached from the Father's good pleasure and purpose in all things, then all we have done is manufacture a Jesus who got caught in the machinery along with us. The blind man was *sent* to Siloam. He was sent there by the one who had been *sent* into the world by His Father. *Sent* denotes purpose. Suffering has a point. And if you have been sent to see the rubble of the tower, then you have been sent to testify as to its meaning of coming judgment. If you have been sent to the pool to wash, you have been sent to testify to your gift of sight, a release from coming judgment. And in either case, you are testifying to the reality of Jesus Christ, Lord and Savior of mankind.

And this is what makes it possible to respond with the thanksgiving that the atheist refuses to offer to God. This is what makes it possible for a father to see to it that his children grow up in an environment dominated and controlled by gratitude. In either case, whether you are dealing with the village atheist or with your own family, make sure everybody gets a good dose. Gratitude declares the meaning of fatherhood like little else can.

I recall one time having finished a job of peeling potatoes for a Thanksgiving feast. I should note here that the way my wife makes mashed potatoes is one of her innumerable glories. Having made my contribution to this process, which stretched and almost exceeded the limit of my culinary abilities, it struck me how grateful I am. Gratitude is as sturdy and as good as the potatoes, and about the only thing I can think of to make the gratitude better would be some butter or gravy. But I shouldn't run ahead.

Thanksgiving Two Ways

There are two kinds of thanksgiving. The first is the harvest home kind of thanksgiving, which even nonbelievers can have some share in (Acts 17:26–27). All of God's common grace is an invitation to grateful response, and once the gift is past, once the gift is actually given, it doesn't take the eye of faith to see its physical presence. The gift is given, and it only takes the ungrateful eye to deny it.

Because Christians are men, they share in the common duty of giving thanks for what is already gathered in the barn, for the wages already earned, for the liberties already secured, for the family already gathered around. The blessings I have received in this category are innumerable—salvation in Christ, a place among God's people, a faithful congregation, parents who know God and who see the world rightly, a wife above rubies, children and grandchildren who all love and fear the Lord, spouses for my children who have brought additional blessings to a family already laden down with them, material plenty, and, as a covenantal representative of all that, a Thanksgiving table groaning under the weight of the bestowed goodness, a table surrounded by laughter, which is just more bestowed goodness.

But there is also thanksgiving by faith, thanksgiving offered for what God *will do* in the future. The hymn rightly says that we don't know what the future holds, but we know who holds the future, and, given the days we are in, it is a great blessing to know by way of corollary who does *not* hold the future—despite all pretensions otherwise. Obama does not, the UN does not, Congress does not, the bureaucrats at Health and Human Services do not, fraudulent global warming scientists do not, the Taliban does not, various trials for terrorists do not, conspiracies do not, conspiracy theorists do not, crushing taxes do not, tax revolts do not, Dick Cheney does not, Noam Chomsky does not, and long gone Ozymandias does not. Neither do things present or things to come, neither height nor depth, nor anything else in all creation. None of them hold the future. This takes us back to the earlier point made about the sovereignty of God over all things.

But the day remains an evil day, and these characters *do* have to be reckoned with. But the way we reckon with them is by walking as God's dearly loved children (Eph. 5:1ff). We are to walk in love (v. 2), and we are to avoid the moral grime that settles in the sludge-pit baths of contemporary entertainment (vv. 3–4). Instead of that loathsome warmth, we are to give ourselves over to what? The answer is the giving of *thanks* (v. 4). This is because the greedmeisters and the whorehounds do not have the inheritance that we do (v. 5). Let no emergent preacher smoothie-man deceive you with his pufferies about diversity and personal choice (v. 6). The wrath of God is coming straight at the children of disobedience, precisely because of their personal choices. So get this straight—the children of light should be overflowing with thanksgiving, because the wrath of God is coming.

Don't stand too close to them (v. 7). Don't partake with them. Walk as children of light (v. 8), the kind of children who give thanks. Bear fruit in accordance with that truth—the fruit being goodness, righteousness, and truth (v. 9). Show the world what God likes (v. 10). His wrath will show them what He hates soon enough. Those people who are groping each other in perverse ways in the darkness don't do anything except expose their shame (vv. 11–12). Light exposes these things, and light does not have to make a lot of noise to do so (vv. 13–14).

So Christians should think about their walk. We should keep our heads up, and look around as we walk (v. 15). The time must not be wasted, because *the days are evil* (v. 16). This thanksgiving that we offer is not because we are deluded about the state of the culture around us—precisely the opposite. We know how bad it is, and we know that we are to understand what the will of God is concerning us (v. 17). What does God want from us *in the evil day*? What does God want from us when the culture is disintegrating around us? He doesn't want us to deaden the pain with anything like wine; He doesn't want us coping with cocaine, Central American herbs, prescription pick-me-ups, or the soporific of an endless chain of stupid movies (v. 18). Neither Huxley's *soma* nor feelies will do for us.

No, the days are evil, so what must we do? We must be filled with the Spirit, and we must sing psalms, hymns, and spiritual songs (v. 19) because our hearts are *full of music*. We must *render thanks* to God the Father in the name of Jesus Christ. Further, we must give thanks for all things in the evil day. All things. For Obama, for Nancy Pelosi, for the lunatics in the Department of Education. *All things*. But is this the Pauline form of Winston coming to love Big Brother? As he would put it, *me genoito*, no way, God forbid. No, let's jump ahead. What else do we do in the evil day? Just look a few verses down. We take on the entire armor of God so that we can stand (as we *fight*) in the evil day (6:10–18). We fight in the evil day, and we fight against the evil. And we fight with a weapon that not one of the evildoers has, and it is secure in our hand. For them to come into possession of that weapon—which is gratitude to God—is tantamount to their surrender. It is a request to be baptized. It is a confession that God is good, Jesus is Lord, the company is kind-hearted, and the potatoes are hot.

In order to guard our children against the unbelief of atheism, we need to be fathers who overflow with gratitude. We need to exhibit this kind of gratitude even when dealing with the realities of pain. Darwin did not fall away because of natural selection; he fell away because his daughter died. If God existed, He "wouldn't let me get hurt this way." The reality of the pain does not make the argument stronger; it only feels strong. In order to protect the family, the father must lead the way in modeling gratitude.

One of the central ways we fight with this weapon is by offering to share it with the enemy. One of the central things we do with this weapon is protect our children with it. Come, we say, and welcome, to Jesus Christ.

Questions to Consider:

1. How is it possible for Christians to identify God with love? What does the Trinity have to do with it?
2. Why are fathers constantly speaking about God, whether they want to be or not?
3. What are the two fundamental sticking points for unbelief?
4. What is the relationship between the collapsed tower of Siloam and the blind man who washed in the pool of Siloam?
5. Why is the argument against God more than a simple problem in logic?

Chapter 6

The Education Axle

Nurture and Admonition

Education is not simply a means of data transfer. It is not reducible to state-certified techniques. Education, when it succeeds, is the result of a child wanting to be like someone else. If you take away the drive train, can you really be surprised that the car won't go? Fathers are essential to any successful school system, and no system of education can successfully compensate for the abdication of fathers.

> *Fathers,* do not provoke your children to anger, but bring them up in the discipline and instruction of the Lord. (Eph. 6:4)

There are two critical things to notice about this requirement. The first is that it requires a Christian education for Christian children, and the second is that this commandment is laid at the feet of *fathers*. Let's take these two points in order.

In the phrase "discipline and instruction," it can actually be difficult to tell which English word is being used for which Greek word, because they are so close in meaning. The two words in the Greek are *paideia* and *nouthesia*. In the ESV, discipline is the rendering for the word *paideia*, a word with very broad implications in the ancient world.[1] The word *nouthesia*, rendered as instruction, was similar, at least in its denotative meaning.

Paideia was, for the ancients, an all-encompassing process, designed to accomplish the successful enculturation of the future citizen. In other words, it was a loaded term. Unlike a simple noun for *chair* or *table*, this was more like the word *democracy* is for us. If we were to discover that a scholar somewhere had written a three-volume study on the word for *chair*, our first, second, and third impulses would be to exhort him to try to get out a little bit more. Ask a girl out. Take her to the movies. Get her a sno-cone. *Something*. But we wouldn't feel this way if we discovered a scholar had written a three-volume study on the word *democracy*. In fact, we might wonder if three volumes would be quite enough. I use this example because I have on my shelves a three-volume study of *paideia* by the great scholar Werner Jaeger.[2] This is not an example of scholarship with no brakes; it is a great example of how some nouns can carry an awful lot of weight and can reward diligent study.

Our word *education* could be used to translate the word *paideia*, but even education could be construed in too narrow a fashion. Everything that is involved in preparing a child today for life tomorrow would have to be included.[3] The word *education* might be limited, in the minds of many, to something that happens between 8:00 a.m. and 3:00 p.m., book-ended by a yellow bus ride both to and from. But *paideia* includes diet, music, entertainment, sports, the whole shebang.

But if *paideia* involves broad enculturation, then a *paideia* "of the Lord" requires a Christian culture. And this means, in its turn, if we do not have a Christian culture, then it is our obligation to build one. We cannot have a Christian *paideia* without Christian culture, and, in the long run, we cannot sustain a Christian culture without a

Christian *paideia*. Conservative Christians today are accustomed to speak about our "culture wars," but this is something of a misnomer. Just as you cannot have tank warfare without tanks, or naval warfare without ships, so we cannot have culture warfare without a culture. And we cannot have a distinctively Christian view of culture unless we have deep commitments to the ideal of a thoroughgoing Christian education.

Paul requires that kind of commitment here, and he assigns the responsibility for it to the *fathers*. Fathers, therefore, are the guardians of culture. Earlier in this book we noted how the basic responsibilities assigned to Adam were those of providing and protecting, cultivating and guarding. These twin responsibilities really come to the fore when we are discussing the task of education. Fathers are responsible to cultivate a biblical view of the world that comes with true education, and they are responsible to guard it against compromise and drift once it is established.

Fathers are responsible to see to it that the transmitters of culture from generation to generation (we call them schools) are in good working order, and that they embody the kind of *paideia* referred to here. In addition, all the other elements of enculturation, iPads included, are also to be under the authority of the lordship of Christ. A father is responsible to lead his children in a way that helps them think biblically about *everything*.

The Great Commandment

One of the loftiest passages in all of Scripture is a passage that is actually about the education of children. It is a charge to fathers to teach their children in all the ways of God, and it is a charge to the children, to the students, to remember what God had done for their fathers. This is the passage in which we find the commandment identified by Jesus Himself as the greatest commandment to be found in all of Scripture. It's a long quote—don't skip to the end and hope I'll sum it up for you. Read it all and read it closely.

> Now this is the commandment—the statutes and the rules—that the LORD your God commanded me to teach you, that you may do them in the land to which you are going over, to possess it, that you may fear the LORD your God, *you and your son and your son's son,* by keeping all his statutes and his commandments, which I command you, all the days of your life, and that your days may be long. Hear therefore, O Israel, and be careful to do them, that it may go well with you, and that you may multiply greatly, as the LORD, *the God of your fathers,* has promised you, in a land flowing with milk and honey.
>
> Hear, O Israel: The LORD our God, the LORD is one. You shall love the LORD your God with all your heart and with all your soul and with all your might. And these words that I command you today shall be on your heart. You shall teach them diligently to your children, and shall talk of them when you sit in your house, and when you walk by the way, and when you lie down, and when you rise. You shall bind them as a sign on your hand, and they shall be as frontlets between your eyes. You shall write them on the doorposts of your house and on your gates.
>
> And when the LORD your God brings you into the land *that he swore to your fathers, to Abraham, to Isaac, and to Jacob,* to give you—with great and good cities that you did not build, and houses full of all good things that you did not fill, and cisterns that you did not dig, and vineyards and olive trees that you did not plant—and when you eat and are full, then take care lest you forget the LORD, who brought you out of the land of Egypt, out of the house of slavery. (Deut. 6:1–12)

We should note that when Jesus quotes from this passage, He adds something to the list. In addition to heart, soul, and might, Jesus says that we are to love the Lord our God with all our *mind*. "And you shall love the Lord your God with all your heart and with all your soul and *with all your mind* and with all your strength" (Mark 12:30). Jesus says that we are to love the Lord our God with all our *brains*—and this would include our math brains, our history brains, our grammar brains, our science brains, and our lunchroom brains. Clearly, what you learn to do with your brains has something to do with education—at least in a decent school it does.

In this great passage on education, the focus is on fathers and sons. When men take the lead in the education of all their children, you will always find a high degree of appreciative involvement from the women. But when women are left holding the bag, what you'll find is a lot of stress, burnout, and frustration, with the men down at the showroom checking out the new speedboats.

True education is not possible apart from a real understanding of what it means to bear the image of God. Again, fathers are responsible to cultivate and maintain this understanding within their homes. Notice how Jesus handles the question about paying taxes to Caesar.

> But Jesus, aware of their malice, said, "Why put me to the test, you hypocrites? Show me the coin for the tax." And they brought him a denarius. And Jesus said to them, "Whose likeness and inscription is this?" They said, "Caesar's." Then he said to them, "Therefore render to Caesar the things that are Caesar's, and to God the things that are God's." (Matt. 22:18–21)

We tend to read this passage as though only the coin had an image on it. But Jesus assumes two different kinds of image bearers. When they ask the famous question about taxes, Jesus asks for the coin in question. When He gets one, He asks whose "likeness and inscription" were on it. They reply that it was Caesar's. Jesus replies that it is lawful then to give to Caesar that which Caesar managed to get his image on. But He doesn't stop there. He says also that we are to render to God the things that are God's. Implied in this is that, just as Caesar had his image on the coins, so also God has His image on . . . what? What are we to render to God and *not* to Caesar? The answer is that which bears God's image, which would include our children. God created us in His image, meaning that we are not permitted to render ourselves to Caesar.

Christian education, therefore, rightly understood, is a means or instrument for rendering our children to God. In the passage from Deuteronomy cited earlier, the children of the covenant were to grow up in an environment dominated by the Word of God. When a father walked with his kids, when they got up, when they drove down the road, when they sat down at the dinner table, they were to talk about what God had said in His Word about the world.

To many, this conjures up images of making pious and suitably long faces in order to talk about anything, all while randomly attaching verses to the subject at hand. All of life is approached the same sad way in which science fair projects are pursued in superficial Christian schools. The student does his research on stars, for example, and does whatever it is he is going to do. When he is done, he runs off to find a concordance to get a verse that has stars in it, and then he attaches *that,* entirely arbitrarily, to his poster board project. "Is not God high in the heavens? See the highest stars, how lofty they are!" (Job 22:12).

In a true Christian education, the Scriptures are not placed on the wall like a picture, for purposes of decoration, but rather are mounted on the wall like a thermostat in order to control the climate of the whole school. I was once told about a Christian school that supposedly had a Christian worldview education because chapel was offered "first thing" in the morning. In this truncated approach, a Christian school is one in which prayers are still legal, and it is acceptable to add a Bible class to the curriculum. But all the other subjects—English, history, math, and so forth—are still taught in just the same way that such classes are taught in all the other schools. It is as though the different subjects are like different shirts drying on the clothesline, and at the Christian school they hang out an extra shirt.

Another illustration of this same kind of problem is to compare the supposedly neutral content of education as a basic substance, like nutritious but flavorless oatmeal, and to treat the distinctive religions and worldviews held by the parents as flavors or condiments. In this view, government schools can dispense the basic knowledge that everybody needs, and then the Hindus, Muslims, Christians, and agnostics can take it home in order to flavor their oatmeal to suit their own tastes.

But education is fundamentally a religious activity. It is an insinuation into a culture, and every culture has a god. All cultures always have a god of the system. With democratic secularism, that god is Demos, the people. Education is therefore a *paideia* that renders service to the true God, or to false ones. The fact that Christians go along with an enculturation in the ways of false gods is not a refutation of the thesis, but is rather more good reason to heed the exhortation of the apostle John to keep ourselves from idols (1 John 5:21). John warns Christians to stay away from idols because it is possible for Christians not to.

In order to fulfill the charge that Paul assigns to fathers, these Christian fathers must come to understand the complete nature of an integrated worldview. A worldview consists of much more than the mere thoughts we think in our heads. That is an important *part* of our worldview, but it is by no means the whole.

Christ the Axle

The Bible says that Christ is the principle of integration. He is the one in whom all things hold together. "And he is the head of the body, the church. He is the beginning, the firstborn from the dead, that in everything he might be preeminent" (Col. 1:18). The word rendered here as "the beginning" is *arche*, referring in this case to the ultimate point of integration. Christ is the Cornerstone. Christ is the Capstone. Christ is the Hinge. Christ is the Apex. Christ is the Axle.

Taking this image of Christ as the axle, imagine for a moment that a worldview has four spokes—a worldview wheel. Two of the spokes are propositional, and two of them are enacted. All of them must be attached to the axle, who is Christ. The two propositional spokes are *catechesis* and *narrative*, and the two enacted spokes are *lifestyle* and *symbolism/ritual*. A father who is overseeing the education of his children must see to it that all four spokes are there and in good working order.

In our postmodern times, it is customary for people to be dismissive of "propositional" truth (usually in favor of narrative), but this is usually an emotional reaction away from what they accuse of being a dry creedalism. However, the problem is not the creed, but rather the creed in isolation from the other elements of a biblical worldview. But before they react too strongly, they should remember that stories are made up of propositions as much as creeds are. For them to reject creeds in favor of narrative, and to do so in the name of rejecting "propositions," is like a man who wanted an omelet instead of three over easy, and who expressed this desire by rejecting the whole idea of eggs. "God from all eternity, did, by the most wise and holy counsel of His own will, freely, and unchangeably ordain whatsoever comes to pass"[4] is a proposition, certainly. But so is "Once upon a time, a little boy named Tommy lived in a gray castle next to the deep blue sea." And "one day the dragon came" is yet *another* proposition. So whether the propositionalism is *dry* depends entirely on how many dragons there are. In the Apostles' Creed there are at least a couple.

Catechesis has to do with how you teach your children to answer the question, "What do you believe?" The (propositional) response is to say, "I believe in God the Father Almighty, Maker of Heaven and earth, and in Jesus Christ His only begotten Son, our Lord . . ."

Narrative answers the questions, "Who are your people, and how did you get here? Where are you going?" Narrative creates a timeline for the students, with an *X* on the timeline that says, "You are here." This is where we came from, this is where we are, and here is the direction we are going.

Lifestyle has to do with your day-to-day customs—how and why you brush your teeth, what your dietary practices are, how you dress, whether or not you are a big techie, and so on. Included here would also be the virtues engendered by the Holy Spirit, directing *how* you do all these things. Are these things done with love, joy, peace, patience, and the remaining fruit of the Spirit (Gal. 5:22–23)?

Symbolism/ritual is a nonverbal way of communicating some of the content of your worldview and your identification with it. Examples of this kind of thing would be crosses on the top of steeples, school uniforms, wedding rings, standing when a woman enters the room, and partaking of bread and wine in a worship service.

We can see how the secularist has all four elements functioning in his worldview. This is the way all worldviews function. He tells us that he believes in evolution and natural selection (*catechesis*). He tells us that our people used to live in medieval superstition until the Enlightenment showed us the way out of that darkness (*narrative*). He insists that men should be allowed to marry men (*lifestyle*). And he fights like the dickens to keep a Christmas crèche from being set up at the county courthouse (*symbolism*).

Returning to the place where we began, Paul tells fathers to provide their children with a *paideia* of the Lord. This *paideia* is to be understood as an all-encompassing reality. What fathers may not do is provide their children with one Christian spoke and three secularist spokes and then call it good. Those three spokes are metric and won't go into our axle.

Worldviews are inescapable. This means that it is not *whether* we will have a worldview, but rather *which* worldview we will have. Not whether but which. This means that when Christian fathers abdicate their responsibilities to provide their children with a Christian *paideia,* it is not as though nothing happens. No, a process of enculturation is going to happen one way or the other. If a Christian father does not teach his children that the dead are raised, someone else is going to teach them that the dead will do no such thing. If he does not teach them that God brought our fathers up out of the land of Egypt, then somebody else is going to teach them that our primate ancestors came down out of the trees somewhere in Africa. If he does not teach them that marriage was intended for one man, one woman, one time, then someone else is going to show them that marriage is a social construct, and as times change, so do the constructs—as evidenced by Adam and Steve here. If he does not teach them to show honor to God by appearing before Him in worship once a week, then someone else is going to deck him out with some tats, droopy trousers, and baseball cap problems. Nature does indeed abhor a vacuum, and when Christian fathers leave a vacuum, someone or something else will in fact fill it.

A father has no business begetting children that he has no intention of feeding. In the same way, a biblical father is responsible for *educating* the children that God gives to him. This education means giving his children an entire world—God's world. The earth is the Lord's and the fullness thereof (Ps. 24:1). This means that education is education that prepares the students for the world as it actually is.

If Christ is not the Lord *of* all, then He is not the Lord *at* all. But if He is, in fact, the Lord of Heaven and earth, then an education that equips someone to live on earth in the light of Heaven has to be an education that takes this lordship into account.

> Therefore God has highly exalted him and bestowed on him the name that is above every name, so that at the name of Jesus every knee should bow, in heaven and on earth and under the earth, and every tongue confess that Jesus Christ is Lord, to the glory of God the Father. (Phil. 2:9–11)

An education that is formally agnostic (which is another way of saying "an education that *pretends* to be agnostic") is pretending that knowledge can be neutral—like the oatmeal we compared it to earlier. It is being assumed that the secular schools do not take a position, one way or the other, when it comes to whether or not Jesus is Lord. But what is actually being said is that *if* He is Lord, then that lordship is irrelevant to the material that will be covered in the course of this education. This pretends to not address the question, all while disingenuously addressing it. To say that Christ is irrelevant to what we are doing is to say, in so many words, that He is *not* Lord.

In contrast to this, consider Abraham Kuyper's famous statement from his inaugural address at the Free University of Amsterdam. "There is not a square inch in the whole domain of our human existence over which Christ, who is Sovereign over all, does not cry: 'Mine!'" If this is true, and it most certainly is, what are the ramifications for education?

When children are growing up in a healthy way, the boys will want to grow up to be like their fathers, and the girls will want to grow up into the kind of women who men like their fathers would want to be with. A common *paideia,* related to Christian culture, grounded in biblical truth, is an essential part of this.

Questions to Consider:

1. Why is education more than a simple matter of data transfer?
2. Why is the word *paideia* not a common noun?
3. What significance to education does Christ's statement about Caesar's coin and image have?
4. What are the four spokes of the "worldview wheel"?
5. What is an inescapable concept?

Chapter 7

Small Father, Big Brother

The Abortion of the Family

Edmund Burke famously wrote about the "little platoons" that make up a free society. But the overweening secular state wants to dissolve all those platoons and wants instead a host of atomistic individuals, the easier for them to manipulate. In contrast to this, strong fathers create a molecular society, with numerous bonds that are not under the control of any state agency whatsoever. A man should honor his wife's loveliness in her fertility, and he must rejoice in the fact that his children will be greeted in this world by breasts full of grace, thinly disguised as milk.[1] This is why the war on marriage and family is no accidental war. The concerted statist war on fathers is not being conducted in spasms of absentmindedness. All that is necessary in order to discern what the strategy is to look at it straight on. But we rarely do this.

The infamous *Roe v. Wade* decision legalizing abortion in the United States has been justly opposed by faithful Christians in the decades since 1973, and it has been rightly opposed on the basis of the horrendous bloodshed—forty million lives and counting. But something else happened in that fateful decision that is rarely seen or commented on, even though the destructive effects have been incalculable. I am referring to the abortion of the idea of legitimate fatherhood.

A decision whether to have an abortion now famously rests between the "woman and her doctor." Who is missing from this? Entirely left out of this life-and-death question is whether or not the woman is married. If she is married, should her husband, the legitimate father of the child in question, have any say in the matter? Left out is the question of whether the covenant of marriage should be taken into account at all when it comes to whether the children of a lawful sexual union live or die. In *Roe*, the Supreme Court in effect determined that every American child is, in the eyes of the court, a covenantal bastard.[2]

The destructive leveling effects of this have been implemented from another direction. At the same time that we have seen legitimate fathers *excluded* from the decision whether or not their sons or daughters will live or die, we have seen illegitimate fathers *included* in the lawsuits surrounding adoption, visitation rights, and so on.

The assault is therefore on the very concept of legal paternity. No child is entitled to the protections of a father. A father who has bound himself in matrimony for life has no more legal say over whether his child lives or dies than some free-range motorcyclist who was in town for just a night or two. In the eyes of the Supreme Court, that vanishing man has the same amount of legal say when it comes to the abortion of his child as a man who has committed himself to remain for life—which is to say, *none*.

The Problem of Men

George Gilder has demonstrated that a sane civic order depends upon taming male sexuality. Left to their own devices, the sexual rhythms of untamed males are the rhythms of a biker gang or a boat full of pirates. Civilization depends on getting men to submit their sexual "Freebird" ethic to a far more stable feminine sexuality. Stable civil order depends upon getting a bit and bridle onto male sexuality. Men must learn, says Gilder, to "shun the consolations of alcohol and leisure, sexual indulgence and flight."[3]

A popular complaint among women is the problem of getting a guy "to commit." Well, sister, you're not the only one. Western culture spent *centuries* teaching men to commit themselves to one woman for life, and in practice this has meant teaching him to commit to his offspring. It has also meant giving him an important role to play in the protection of those children, and in his provision for them. *Roe* wiped that out. It doesn't matter if a man commits or not anymore; our legal system has determined that such commitments are irrelevant. But we are now discovering that male commitments were much more important than we thought.

Gilder puts it this way:

> Marriage asks men to give up their essential sexuality only as part of a clear scheme for replacing it with new, far more important, and ultimately far more sexual roles: husband and father. Without these roles, a woman can bear a child, but the man is able only to screw. He can do it a lot, but after his first years it will only get him unthreaded, and in the end he is disconnected and alone. In his shallow heats and frustrations, he all too often becomes a menace to himself and his community.[4]

We can and should take issue with Gilder's notion of "*essential* sexuality," as though this were a function of some distant evolutionary past instead of being a function of our race's fall into sin and rebellion. Man was created by God to be in fellowship with God and with his spouse. In other words, contra Rousseau and his unwitting popularizers, man was created for civilization. It was our rebellion against this created order that caused everything to come unstuck for us.

Nevertheless, even if we take exception to Gilder's language about essential sexuality, the results come out the same. Men now are sinners, and men now chafe under the responsibilities of civilized maturity. Men like to head down the road with yet one more farmer's-daughter story. This means that if men are not given a constructive role in society, then they will easily opt for the destructive one. "Masculinity is no myth . . . marriage largely depends upon it, and . . . civilization depends on marriage."[5] That destructive role may be active, as with criminal activity, or passive, as what happens when men simply disappear.

So when the state does this kind of thing—disrupting and seeking to eliminate the constructive role for men that was painstakingly built over the course of centuries—we should ask a very basic question. What's in it for them? Why would they want men to opt for a destructive role? To answer this question, we don't have to believe that every last state functionary is malevolent, cackling over their evil policies as though they were Sauron's henchmen of Mordor. No, a lot of them believe they are spreading sweetness and light; a lot of them believe their own propaganda. They believe the state actually is compassionate.

But at some level, *someone* understands what is happening. And at this level, the answer is that men are easier to compete with when they are detached from their families. Says Gilder, "Achieving economic planning, income equality, bureaucratic rationality, and sexual liberation—the retrenchment of religion and suppression of sex roles—requires a totalitarian state."[6] Not only does it *require* a totalitarian state to achieve these things, achieving such perverse ends *results* in a totalitarian state. There is a self-reinforcing feedback loop here. The more men act badly, the more obvious it is that the state must restrain them. The more they are restrained by force, the more power the state has. "When we weaken the family unit, we become vulnerable to other forces," writes Kathleen Parker. "Incrementally, government fills the void once occupied by parents."[7]

Conversely, if men are responsible, sober, hard-working members of their local communities—*self*-restrained—this creates pockets of personal responsibility that the state does not easily control.

A society filled with atomistic individuals is like a sack full of disconnected and well-oiled BBs. It has no internal structure, no internal skeleton. The state can push in however it wants, and can expect no pushback or resistance. But if there is a molecular structure, independent of the state, then everything is not quite as subject to manipulation. But if we want that molecular structure, then we must have *fathers*. If the state wants to get rid of those pesky molecular structures, then they must get rid of fathers. In order to get rid of those fathers, they have been offering bribes, mostly of a sexual nature, in order to seduce men back into a state of primitive irresponsibility.

G. K. Chesterton says that free love, sexual laxity, is the first and most obvious bribe that can be offered to a slave. The freedoms for which the Left—ever friendly to the burgeoning state—agitates are the kind that can be indulged in a six-by-eight prison cell. You can look at porn in such a cell, you can fornicate in a cell, you can smoke dope, and so on. In contrast, the kind of liberties that conservatives want people to have are the liberties that allow them to move around the country, settle wherever they want, start a business, make money, and most important, keep that money in order to feed their families. Most real liberty does not even appear on the state's radar screen. People are just out there on their own, you know, *doing* stuff. Says Chesterton,

> The family is older than the State; and this means that agreement is older than coercion. . . . The family is primarily supposed to rest

> upon consent. . . . It is for this reason that the father of a family has never been called "the king of the house" or "the priest of the house," or again, "the pope of the house." His power was not dogmatic or definite enough for that. He was called "the head of the house." The man is the head of the house, while the woman is the heart of the house.[8]

The family is older than the state. The family rests upon love and not upon coercion. Consequently, whenever possible, the claims of the state should give way before those of the family.

But in order for this to happen, the foundation of all true government must first be established. That foundation is self-government, self-control. There are three governments among men that God created directly. He established the family when He gave Eve to Adam (Gen. 2:22; Matt. 19:6). He established the civil magistrate (Rom. 13:1–2). And of course, He established the church (Eph. 4:11–12). But all three of these forms of human society come apart in our hands without self-government. And when we don't have self-government, it is principally among the *men* that we don't have it.

Boys will be boys, and you know where that leads.

Targeted Fathers

Even though self-government is necessary for all three forms of government to be free and *responsible* government, the state—having recourse to coercion—can pretend that it is less necessary for them. The family and church are nothing without voluntary willingness to be part of it. This is also true of the state, but less obvious. The state can knock heads for a while in a way that keeps up appearances. This is why the encroachments of the state deliberately target fathers.

Self-control is a fruit of the Spirit, and so it is the Spirit who must teach men that they have an important role to play—a role that requires them to be in full possession of their wits, as well as to possess one functional backbone. And the Spirit works with the whole man—He does not just bring about self-control by means of sporadic mystic fits. The Spirit teaches, and one of the things He teaches a man is that his manhood has a *point*. His capacity for fatherhood is there for a reason. When a man picks up that responsibility with the intention of being serious about it, he soon finds himself living as a pillar in the family, in the church, and in the community. He also finds himself in conflict with anyone in those institutions who is seeking to profiteer off of male irresponsibility.

Paul Vitz notes how father hunger provides a real opportunity for demagogues:

> Recently, much has been written about the absence of fathers in American families. Presumably, this widespread defective fathering will cause an increase in contemporary skeptical attitudes toward God. But it may also result in equally widespread "father hunger" which could manifest itself in a variety of ways, such as a growth in cults and support for political demagogues.[9]

This is quite true, but we have also been emphasizing that demagogues are going to do what they can to *further* such widespread father hunger. It is not as though this father hunger is happening as some kind of a fluke and then the state accidentally fills that void. If a certain kind of soil grows a plant that some unscrupulous men want to have, it is not long before they figure out how to fertilize for that kind of soil in order to be able to harvest that kind of plant. If they like the crop, some men become farmers.

You get more of what you subsidize and less of what you penalize. Over time, what you subsidize and what you penalize reveal what you are actually after. What does our government subsidize? If a girl in the inner city gets pregnant, the state will offer to take care of her *provided she does not marry the father.* We then scratch our heads over the epidemic of illegitimacy we have created when we are subsidizing that illegitimacy. And when a man takes responsibility, marries a woman, starts a business, begins to employ other people, we make sure to fine him heavily and throw in a bunch of regulations to keep the hassle factor high.

The only way out is for men to return to God. "The way of deliverance from human authoritarianism is the rediscovery of divine authority," writes Thomas Smail.[10] If we want deliverance from the false savior of the state, we are going to have to appeal to a real Savior—and there is only one of those. When men return to God, they quickly discover that God calls them to reassume the role designed for them, and He equips them for that role. When a man assumes his assigned and proper role as husband and father, and he takes his responsibilities with all biblical seriousness, he is establishing his family as a small fortress that the arrogant state has real trouble meddling with. G. K. Chesterton says:

> But in most normal cases of family joys and sorrows, the State has no mode of entry. It is not so much that the law should not interfere, as that the law cannot. Just as there are fields too far off for law, so there are fields too near; as a man may see the North Pole before he sees his own backbone.[11]

As necessary as this response is, it is equally important that it not be a reaction. Something crucial that my own father taught me was "act, never react." When you react to things, the thing you are reacting to is still in control of the situation. God calls husbands and fathers to act on principle, and not to react against statist excesses. This is because reaction breeds new excesses, and that is precisely what we do not need.

If we discover ourselves reacting to a state that claims to have a rightful interest in *everything*, we are being very foolish if we respond by saying that they have a rightful interest in *nothing*. We live in an era when the state *claims* to have expertise that hovers on the edges of omniscience. But if fathers react blindly to such claims, we will soon find ourselves dealing with fathers who are just as absolutist and foolish as the state was being. It is not the case that fathers can do everything better for their family than outsiders. Brain surgery in the garage comes to mind. Fathers have particular duties assigned to them by God, and it is not "reaction" to pick up those duties. At the same time, it is not obedience to look at what others are doing and mindlessly do the opposite.

Civic Fatherlessness

In these days of grasping statism, it has been very easy for freedom-loving fathers to say that their fatherly duties require them to retire to the country, raise chickens, and make their own soap. But does true fatherhood really have to disconnect from the grid? While it is perfectly acceptable for some families to pursue their agrarian rhythms in peace, to insist on this for everybody is to confuse principles and methods. And to declare radical independence from our nation as it currently stands is to do the same. Far from manifesting true fatherhood coming into its own, this is actually a new form of the same disease that is currently afflicting us.

Hard libertarianism and anarchism are functions of what might be called civic fatherlessness. Just as the antitheist regards the eternality of the Father as tyrannical on the face of it, so also the hard libertarian regards any civic authority whatsoever as something to chafe the soul. It is not a coincidence that many political libertarians are also atheists.

Within this paradigm, all political authority is based on coercion, straight-up, and since coercion is (obviously) bad, then at best we should regard political authority as a necessary evil, and at worst tyranny to be thrown off. Those who are more eschatologically minded long for the day when the state withers, or blows up—or *something*—so that every man can sit fatherless under his own fig tree. This view assumes that the only possible justification for civil authority is some sort of pragmatism, and when we grow past the need for such pragmatic expedients, then we will no longer have any presidents or kings. We will have grown out of our need for civil fathers, or so the pipe dream goes.

But as I write this, I am in my late fifties, and my father is in his eighties. He is still very much an authority in my life, and the respect I owe to him is truly significant. But suppose I were telling this to a libertarian friend, and he said that the only reason I still felt this way was because I was afraid of getting a spanking. That would obviously be ridiculous, even though there is a grain of truth there—but a grain of truth that arrived about five decades late. Godly fathers do establish their authority by love and discipline, but the house they are building is not the same as the scaffolding. When a son grows to maturity, the scaffolding comes down and the fatherly authority remains. We do not grow *out of* our need for discipline by our authorities without growing *into* something else. And what we grow into is not radical autonomy with a fatherless vacuum above us.[12]

Scripture tells little children that their honor of their father and mother is rendered through obedience (Eph. 6:1). When children are grown, the honor is still required, but it is rendered through different means: they are supposed to honor father and mother through financial support (Mark 7:11–12). The surrounding duties are different because the central duty is the same.

An unruly and ungodly people must be ruled in a rough-and-tumble fashion (1 Tim. 1:9). But as their capacity for self-government grows (which is only possible through the gospel), they discover that in their maturity they can start to see things about their rulers that were not clear to them before.

> And the LORD made Solomon very great in the sight of all Israel and *bestowed on him such royal majesty* as had not been on any king before him in Israel. (1 Chron. 29:25)

> *The God of Israel has spoken;*
> *the Rock of Israel has said to me:*
> *When one rules justly over men,*
> *ruling in the fear of God,*
> *he dawns on them like the morning light,*
> *like the sun shining forth on a cloudless morning,*
> *like rain that makes grass to sprout from the earth.*
> (2 Sam. 23:3–4)

And of course, in our day, when we really are dealing with various tyrannies that do not have the fear of God as a political consideration at *all*, the key phrase to focus on in the previous passage is "when one rules justly over men, ruling in the fear of God." What we have now is a ganglion of thieves "ruling impudently over men, ruling in the greasy oil slick arrogance of man." But even so, we still salute the uniform, as Paul did with Ananias (Acts 23:3–5).

In John's great vision of the New Jerusalem, one of the things that happens is that kings bring their honor and glory into it (Rev. 21:24). This was also foretold by the prophet Isaiah: "Kings shall be your foster fathers, and their queens your nursing mothers. With their faces to the ground they shall bow down to you, and lick the dust of your feet. Then you will know that I am the LORD; those who wait for me shall not be put to shame" (49:23).

When it comes to responsible civic liberty, Christian men have to learn how to hate every form of despotic tyranny. But they must do this in faith and not in reaction. The Holy Spirit is the giver of liberty (2 Cor. 3:17), but the Holy Spirit is *not* the creator of fatherless autonomy. The lover of political liberty should long for the day when kings will be *foster fathers* for the church, not for the day when kings and presidents will finally "get theirs."

Another way of saying this is that liberty is to be defined by God and not by what irritates me. James tells us that the Scriptures are the perfect law of liberty (James 1:25). Liberty is not an abstraction but rather what we enjoy when we order our lives in accordance with the way God instructs us to live. If we have three governments established by God, then we should actually understand them as three departments, three ministries.

The family is to be the ministry of health, education, and welfare. The state is to be the ministry of justice. The church is to be the ministry of Word and sacrament. And all of it is to be under the authority of the Lord Jesus. In different eras, each of these ministries has gotten above its appointed station. In times of patriarchal tribalism, the family overgrew its bounds. In the medieval period, the church did. In our day, the state is the principal culprit. But if we get them back in balance, we can call it Christendom 2.0. Or perhaps a better name for it would be mere Christendom.

Questions to Consider:

1. In what way was *Roe v. Wade* involved in the abortion of the family?
2. How are men behaving badly a setup for totalitarianism?
3. What is the difference between atomistic society and molecular society?
4. You get more of what you subsidize and less of what you penalize. How is this significant in the growth of the state?
5. How does a child's duty to honor father and mother mature and change as he grows up and leaves home?

Chapter 8

Escaping the Pointy-Haired Boss

Free Men, Free Markets

When we seek to address the relationship of a man (and his family) to the modern corporate structure of modern business in America, one of the first things we must do is define our terms. In this instance, we must do it because we tend to think we live in a capitalist society. It would be nice if we did, and we have often been *told* that we do, but we actually live in a society that is simply less non-capitalist than a lot of others. As a result, Chesterton's famous quip about Christianity becomes applicable to the economics of free markets. "It has not been tried and found wanting, it has been found difficult and not tried."

As Christian fathers find themselves isolated in a Dilbert cubicle of some description, with a hard hour-long commute on either end, driving either toward or away from a very lonely and isolated family, it is not surprising that more and more men are increasingly dissatisfied with the whole setup. The hit sitcom *The Office* is popular because when all else fails, you can always laugh at your pain. But laughter (and all manner of other diversions) should not distract fathers from thinking through the problems here. The attempts of corporate America to separate men from their wives and children seem perverse and deliberate. We call it *work* for a reason; but this is ridiculous. Because we are constantly and incessantly told that this *is* American capitalism, we should not be surprised that more and more Christians are increasingly dissatisfied with that capitalism.

What we are actually dealing with in America today is not true capitalism. It's a virulent form of crony capitalism, what I have elsewhere described as crapitalism. In other words, when big business and big government conspire to regulate the business climate (and always in the name of correcting or reforming abuses), the inevitable result is that choices and options for individual citizens start vanishing. What is usually overlooked is the fact that the abuses being reformed are the direct result of the previous wave of reform. The fact remains that we are not competent enough to run the economy of a midsized town, much less the economy of a great nation. Nevertheless, our tangle of regulations, bad ideas, and government-granted competitive advantages has become our country's form of capitalism, and so it is not surprising that capitalism is getting a bad rap.

Because this way of life seems as though it is for the birds, and because socialism and other forms of collectivism have received their (deserved) measure of opprobrium from Christians, a number of us have started to look for a third way. Some think they have found it in an approach called distributism, popularized by Hilaire Belloc and G. K. Chesterton. This, combined with an agrarian romanticism, has led some Christian men to think that they *have* to get out of the city and that their fatherly duty must somehow involve three acres and a cow.

Under socialism, the means of production are owned or controlled by the state. Under (plutarchic) capitalism, the means of production are owned by a handful of hyper-wealthy individuals, whose names all rhyme with Daddy Warbucks. In contrast to this, Chesterton says that "too much capitalism does not mean too many capitalists, but too few capitalists." So Chesterton's idea is to "distribute" the means of production as widely as possible. It would be tempting to adopt this view simply because Chesterton liked it, but we have to do a little more spade work than that.

The whole matter can actually be tackled by addressing one basic question. Granted the need to distribute the means of production to as many people as we can, how is the distribution to be accomplished? Assuming we all think it would be swell were this to happen, *who* is to do it? There are two options before us. The first is the way of coercion, which comes naturally to the human heart, especially the hearts of fixers and reformers. We see something that needs fixing, and so we pick up a cudgel to set about our reforms. When our reforming crusade is over, everybody has three acres and a cow. But if we turn our reforming backs away for a minute, the fellow up the road has six acres and two cows, and another fellow down the road at the tavern is crying about it in his beer. In order to keep this pie dough rolled flat and even, you have to hover over it with a rolling pin.

And of course, this is nothing but coercive socialism with decentralized versus centralized tastes, something of which Chesterton would hardly approve in the end.

So the other way of distributing these means of production, if there is one, has to be noncoercive.[1] How could that work? We could argue (and I *would* argue) that we could accomplish this distribution of the means of production by what we *refuse* to do, and by what powers of collusion we *prevent* between monopolistic big business and big government. How might microbreweries making

quality beer prosper? How might we increase their number? Well, for starters, we could eliminate the hammerlock deal that the big beer makers have with the government.[2] In other words, the only thing we need to coercively prevent is growth in the powers of coercion. I am all for this, but it now turns out that this distributism is nothing more than genuine free-market capitalism.

If fathers want to be closer to their families—and it is a good thing that they do—then there must be certain economic realities that allow for it. After the War Between the States, the logic of the Industrial Revolution was a *centralizing* logic. "The American father, locked into tightening business patterns, was less and less likely to be at home," writes Ann Douglas; "before the Civil War, for example, he usually went back to his house for lunch; after it, he was more likely not to."[3] But history, like a meandering river, can take some surprising turns. The Digital Revolution has been one of those turns.

I am a pastor of a church located up in the chimney of Idaho. For point of reference, there are more trees than people. My point is that we are off the beaten path. And yet, over the years, we have had many families successfully relocate here because the father was able to telecommute. He could keep his job in California, say, by working online and taking an occasional trip to headquarters just to remind him what everybody looks like down there. This is now frequent enough to be routine, but thirty years ago it was a stark impossibility.

It turns out the means of production *have* been getting distributed, and not because somebody passed a law making them do it. The fewer laws and regulations of industry we have, the more of this we will see. There are many examples of this kind of thing, but I will just point to a handful of them. In the seventies I was part of a band that recorded an album. In order to do this, we had to rent a studio containing many thousands of dollars' worth of equipment.

Within the last year I bought an iPad and purchased an app for it that contains a recording studio that can do far *more* than that old clunky expensive studio could, and I bought the whole studio for around five bucks.

I also used to be involved in making books in the pre-desktop publishing days. There was a shop downtown where you could have your file typeset. You would then edit it, have it done again, cut up the pages with scissors, apply wax to the back of those pages, and put them on layout sheets, hopefully straight. This arduous process was itself a radical decentralization from the way it had been previously. Now, with a mouse in my right hand, I can do all that and more—click, click, click.

All this was done by the power of markets. Now even though no economy is (as of yet) as free as it could be, it is possible to compare relative degrees of freedom. Certain states have more economic opportunity (Texas), while others have a great deal less (California). Nations are the same way. Economic liberty is not wired to an on/off switch, but rather is connected to a dimmer switch. The more liberty there is, the more means of production will be spread across the populace without coercion.

Free markets are voluntary exchanges, unmarred by violence or threats of violence. The only thing the government should do is define weights and measures and enforce the basic rules of the game—straightforward rules that we should be able to write down on a 3 x 5 index card. The rules should be basic things like a prohibition of fraud and theft. "Thou shalt not steal"—stuff like that.

Bring this back to the basic concerns of fathers. Fathers need true economic liberty in order to really provide for their families. They ought not to listen to the blandishments of the regulators who promise that they can provide by governmental fiat. Such promises are lies, and at the end of the day, fathers are still trying to provide for their families, but now under a heavy burden of regulations and taxes.

So the real question has to do with who is in charge of the distribution. Who moves this property from here to there? If this happens because some functionary or bureaucrat decides that *you* have too much, and *he* has too little, then the whole exercise is simply legalized pillage, of which we have seen too much already these last two centuries. If the redistribution is done by free and untrammeled markets, then we are, as an intelligent economist might say, cooking with propane.

The problem is that we don't trust free markets because we don't trust God. Adam Smith wrote about an invisible hand that functioned for the general good—so long as nobody officious got in there and started messing with things. What happens is that somebody makes a pile, and the envious outsiders think that he no doubt got that wealthy by dirty deeds of one kind or another. So the envious set up a clamor for reform, and the politicians oblige. But as soon as the new reform laws are in place, still smoking hot, the fat cats (who have, as it turns out, enough money for lawyers and lobbyists) make their move. And thus it is that the regulatory agency created by this reform legislation is manned by a scurvy lot, related to the fat cats by both blood and marriage. Enough time passes for additional problems to develop, people start yelling again, and the whole process is repeated.

But there *is* an invisible hand that governs these things when left alone, and wise Christians know that it is the hand of the Lord Jesus. If we want to prevent the development of a plutocracy (as we should), then the very best way to do it is to leave everybody alone. If we do that, we will discover, to the delight of everybody but the busybodies and fussers, that God is a distributist—but only so long as He is the one doing the distributing.

We want to steer things so that we can see acceptable outcomes in what (to us) are acceptable time frames. In short, we don't want to trust. We want to govern in accordance with what we believe are "scientific" laws of economics, but we just make a hash of it. In reality, there is only one scientific economic law—thou shalt not steal.

The Economic Liberation of Fathers

So what does this have to do with fathers? If fathers are to be liberated from their confinement cells in corporate America, then they must pray and labor for free markets. They must also vote for them. Men who want to be providing fathers in a way that does not sever them from meaningful contact with their families must pray and work for a free society characterized by free markets. But this is only possible if the gospel has already created free men. Men who are enslaved to their lusts and petty envy will always be chumps enough to be easily manipulated by the rising plutocrats. But men who earn their own livings and who refuse to take money that was extorted from others at the point of the tax collector's gun are men who are the only basis of any free society worth the name.

In order for this to work in a way that blesses society, men must be self-disciplined and sacrificial. Without this true masculinity, the free market just gives college dropouts a mechanism for selling pot, or porn-mongers an excuse to supply a product for the ever-increasing demands of lust. So free markets depend on free men, and free men depend on the gospel.

Some readers might find this a little bit too "conservative" for them, but that's all right. I don't mean to sound excessively partisan, and I know this already sounds like it is slightly to the left of King Arthur, and that is with me holding back. But unless the Tea Party folks strike you as a well-meaning band of right-wing Trotskyites, you have not yet grasped how much personal responsibility and liberty I am talking about.

An essential part of this process is the realization that the problems won't be fixed in Washington. In order to get anywhere on the subject of work and vocation, we have to go back to the point where we lost our bearings. One of the places where our loss of the ideas of true liberty is most obvious is in the concept of *vocation*. Authority flows to those who take responsibility, and each father taking responsibility for his vocation under God is an important part of the reformation we need.

Work As a Calling

We must begin with an accurate statement of our problem. Many glorious truths were recovered in the Reformation, and one of them was the doctrine of vocation. Unfortunately, this is part of our Protestant heritage that we have shamefully neglected, and have almost lost.[4] One of the principal indications that we have lost this doctrine is that we nowadays speak easily and readily of "full-time Christian work," as though there were anything else for a Christian to do. The reestablishment of two "holiness" layers of occupations in Christendom has been a terrible loss.

> The Lord said to Moses, "See, I have called by name Bezalel the son of Uri, son of Hur, of the tribe of Judah, and I have filled him with the Spirit of God, with ability and intelligence, with knowledge and all craftsmanship, to devise artistic designs, to work in gold, silver, and bronze, in cutting stones for setting, and in carving wood, to work in every craft." (Ex. 31:1–5)

When the word of the Lord came to Moses, a particular man was *called* by name out of the tribe of Judah. His name was Bezalel, and the Lord filled him with the Spirit of God. This is the first instance of the Bible describing someone as filled with the Spirit. And what were the indications of the Spirit's filling? They were wisdom, understanding, knowledge, and craftsmanship, which gave him the ability to do cunning work with his hands—as a goldsmith, a silversmith, a worker in brass, as a jeweler (or possibly a mason), a woodworker, along with any other similar work. So when the Spirit descends to fill a man for the first time in the Bible, He surprisingly does not choose to do so upon a theologian reading a big, fat scroll. He does do that also, but *later.*

The important thing here is that Bezalel was called. The Latin verb that means "to call" is *vocare,* from which we get our word *vocation,* or *calling.* This is not meant to disparage the importance of a call to the mission field or the ministry—of course not. But we have to understand that *all* Christians are called, and are called to labor self-consciously and faithfully in their calling, whether it is law, real estate, carpentry, medicine, brick-laying, shop-keeping, writing novels or songs, digging latrines, or planting trees. All of God is in all of it.

We must fix it in our minds that God is in everything and works through everything. This means that Christ is hidden in the artisan, and Christ is hidden in the customer. Christ is hidden in the one behind the counter, and He is hidden in the one in front of the counter. He is hidden in the dentist, and hidden in the patient in the chair.

First, God provides *for us* through means. We benefit from the work of the farmer, the fertilizer salesman, the trucker, the grocery store clerk, and the dairyman; and when we bow our heads to thank God for the breakfast cereal, we are thanking Him for His work *in all of these people,* whether they know Him or not. We receive from God through the work of others. We acknowledge this when we pray for our daily bread (Matt. 6:11). We know that God is working in and through all things (Rom. 8:28), and this includes countless daily kindnesses. When we thank the Lord for the cereal, we should know that we are thanking Him for the whole supply chain and not just for the full bowl in front of us.

Second, Christ receives *from us* as we work in each of our vocations. God gratefully *receives* from us through the work we do for others. "Lord, when did I ever give you hot french fries when You were famished?" "Don't you remember? It was that time at the drive-through window." This is the other side of vocation. God keeps track of every cup of cold water (Matt. 10:42), and He reckons *everything* we do for others as done to Him (Matt. 25:34–46).

This means that Christ is hidden in our vocation, and He is hidden in our neighbor. He is hidden in the businessman and hidden in the customer. We are to discover Him there with the eye of faith. We were created for work (Gen. 2:15) and are called to work diligently six days out of seven (Ex. 20:9–11). We are to render all our work to Christ, and not just to the boss when he is present. "Whatever you do, work heartily, as for the Lord and not for men" (Col. 3:23). And we are to *receive* all the work done for us as a gift from Jesus Himself (Matt. 6:11). The mother gives milk to the child, but who fills her breasts with milk in the first place? When the farmer first planted the wheat, he did not know he was making milk for the baby. And Christ is in all of it.

But we have to consider what this understanding of vocation does not mean. All lawful work is full of glory, but it is a glory apprehended by faith. This faith does not necessarily mean that a Christian carpenter pounds nails differently than an unregenerate carpenter (pointy end up, say). But it does mean that he should understand the meaning of what he does, and, over time, this should result in differences in craft competence. In cultures heavily influenced by the gospel, the buildings should fare better in earthquakes than in societies governed by graft and corruption.

Neither should this doctrine be taken as an excuse to become a one-trick pony. A man's vocation is varied and extends to every aspect of his life. This means that a father is not only called to be, say, a software designer, but also called to be a son, a student, a husband, a brother, a citizen, a churchman, and one who puts model ships into bottles. Incidentally, for parents, this means that education should be equipping their child for his or her vocation in this *broad* sense, not the narrow sense. And this, also incidentally, is the meaning of a liberal arts education.

Vocation is not a talisman against worldly difficulties. Americans love "three steps to automatic success," but that is not what the Scriptures promise. Diligence in this way of thinking will generally result in long-term satisfaction with what a man does—instead of the constant flitting from job to job that is so common in our day—but we shouldn't think that God-given changes are a sign that something is necessarily wrong. And neither should we think that vocation means we will just float through the work day—the diapers can really stink, the customers can be unreasonably irate, the promised shipments can be subject to exasperating delays. Rain falls on the just and the unjust (Matt. 5:45). And Christ is in all of it.

As we seek to live in the will of God, we must be mindful of His revealed will for all Christians. After that, we should evaluate on the basis of three criteria—what are our abilities, our opportunities, and our desires? When all three line up, then we should go for it. "The heart of man plans his way, but the LORD establishes his steps" (Prov. 16:9).

A treatment of this subject would be grossly deficient if we did not quote Luther at some point. His wonderful grasp of vocation, the most heavenly and *earthy* of truths, was remarkable. "God Himself milks the cows through the vocation of the milkmaid."

Holy Ambition

When we learn this, really learn it, we are humbled. And this opens the door for godly ambition. In order to work as God really calls us to work, we have to do it the way Eric Liddell ran—in a way in which we feel God's pleasure. And this means that we have to learn how to think rightly about ambition. The first step is to stop waiting for others to provide you with "a job." The world doesn't owe you a job. I have many times reminded men that when the first settlers got here to Idaho, there were *absolutely no jobs*. There was a lot of work to do, but no jobs. So we first check the impulse to have the government or some big corporation provide for us. The second is to recover the concept of vocation. And the third is to become *ambitious* with that vocation.

> *Do you see a man skillful in his work?*
> *He will stand before kings;*
> *he will not stand before obscure men.* (Prov. 22:29)

Fathers who want to provide for their families should want to provide far more than just a paycheck. They should also be striving, in their labors, to be providing an example of what it means to drive for excellence. Dave Harvey, in his admirable study of ambition, says this: "Humility, rightly understood, shouldn't be a fabric softener on our aspirations."[5] As Jonathan Edwards, C. S. Lewis, and John Piper have shown, each in his generation, we were created by God in order to desire. Desire is not wicked or evil. When our race was created, the world was full of good things to be desired, and God gave them to us. The Lord gave it all to us, and what He gave was very good (Gen. 1:29–31).

So the question of virtue does not hinge upon whether you seek your happiness, which in this case would be through vocational satisfaction. Everyone seeks happiness, and that's the way it is. Virtue is based on *what* makes you happy, not *whether* something makes you happy. But suppose you sought to disprove my point by adopting an extreme stoical outlook, in order to show me that not everybody is motivated by the "pursuit of happiness," as I am so glibly maintaining. We are not put in this world for pleasure alone, you might say, and then add that you intend to do your raw duty out to the utter frozen limit. This would not really throw me. I would shrug my shoulders and say, "Whatever makes you happy."

Every person always acts in line with his or her strongest desire. Our virtue is measured by what we desire, not whether we desire. It is not possible for a finite, sentient creature to choose what he is not choosing. Suppose that in order to illustrate this point I offer a man a bowl of bugs to eat, and he declines. Suppose further that I goad him by saying that I guess we do choose things in line with our strongest desire. Suppose I press him to the point where he grabs the bowl of bugs and starts swallowing them whole. Has this principle changed? Not at all. He is still acting in line with his strongest desire, which is now apparently to win the argument.

Grasping this point is essential to a right understanding of a father's ability to provide for his family truly. A man must want a vocation that serves his family in a way that honors God and, having chosen that vocation, he must be ambitious with, in, and through it.

> He will render to each one according to his works: to those who by patience in well-doing *seek for glory and honor* and immortality, he will give eternal life; but for those who are self-seeking and do not obey the truth, but obey unrighteousness, there will be wrath and fury. (Rom. 2:6–8)

If some folks at church asked a young man—who was on the edge of graduating from college—what he planned to do, they would probably be taken aback if he replied that he was going to seek glory and honor. They might have expected a more pedestrian reply about dentistry, or they might have expected a more spiritual-sounding reply about missions. But *whatever* he chooses, it will be in search of glory. What distinguishes a good man from a bad one is what he considers to be glorious. Does he let *God* define that word?

Your actual pursuits are a running scoreboard. They reveal what you actually prize.[6] You do what you want to do. The glory you pursue is the glory that you think is actually glorious. This is an inescapable concept—it is not whether a man will pursue glory, but which glory he will pursue.

But Christians are still (understandably) suspicious about ambition. Can't this sort of thing go terribly wrong? Well, of course it can, but there is also a parable about burying a talent in a handkerchief (Luke 19:20). *Lack of* ambition can go terribly wrong also. Has no one ever lost anything precious through timidity, hesitation, or cowardice?

Nevertheless, those who are concerned about the perils of ambition do have a point. There *is* a kind of selfish ambition that the Bible rejects out of hand. When selfish ambition takes root, all kinds of corruption will follow.

> Who is wise and understanding among you? By his good conduct let him show his works in the meekness of wisdom. But if you have bitter jealousy *and selfish ambition* in your hearts, do not boast and be false to the truth. This is not the wisdom that comes down from above, but is earthly, unspiritual, demonic. For where *jealousy and selfish ambition* exist, there will be disorder and every vile practice. (James 3:13–16)

So a lot of Christians think the game is not worth the candle. If this can go wrong so terribly (and it can), then it is best not to try.

But this overlooks one thing: what we were created for. The servant who buried his money in the ground thought he was playing it safe, but he actually was not. He thought he was sticking close to the shore, but he was not. The shore is Christ, not some sort of emotional conservatism.

This is why our ambitions must be converted the same way the rest of a man is—through the death, burial, and resurrection of Christ. Death is the ultimate detox center. It purifies everything. So, in order to be a clean ambition, it must be a resurrected ambition. Any other way, it will corrupt everything it comes in contact with. If it has not been mortified, ambition will destroy a man. If it has not been mortified, then *lack* of ambition will destroy a man.

The right kind of surrender means that we will be open to God's timing. When God delays our ambitions, it is not because He is saying no, but because those delays help shape who we are becoming. "How we live when ambitions are delayed significantly shapes who we become."[7] If God had given us everything right out of the blocks, what would that have done to us? Our ambition needs to be purified, and that is one of the things that waiting does for us. Real ambition can stand the wait.[8] This is particularly true when we are talking about vocational *ambition*. You pay your dues and you wait. "The Lord is good to those who wait for him" (Lam. 3:25).

Jesus doesn't tell us to avoid the seats of honor at weddings. He teaches us the right way to get *into* them (Luke 14:8–10). He doesn't tell us to rip out the chief seats in the synagogues (Mark 12:39); He tells us not to *love* them in the wrong way. He tells us not to grasp after honors for ourselves. In fact, being in love with honor from others (without reference to God) is something that prevents us from being able to trust in Him. "How can you believe, when you receive glory from one another and do not seek the glory that comes from the only God?" (John 5:44). But if we trust in Him, if we love Him, as Augustine put it, we may do as we please. This is why Scripture says, "Delight yourself in the LORD, and he will give you the desires of your heart" (Ps. 37:4). This is why it also says, "But seek first the kingdom of God and his righteousness, and all these things will be added to you" (Matt. 6:33). Shouldn't men desire what Jesus says they should desire?

The way up is down. This is what is meant by true ambition's path. How clearly do we see the fact that Jesus humbled Himself?[9] Being ambitious to get low is a great purifier. Going high without getting low is corruption. Getting low and staying low is unbelief. So a humility that refuses to be raised up, that refuses to receive God's promises to humility, is not really humility.[10] To be ambitious in God's world means embracing God's way of getting there. It also means embracing God's way of not staying where you are.

One of the temptations Christian men face is the temptation of thinking that all the obligations attending fatherhood are wrapped up in the simple task of "breadwinning." But there is a trap. Providing the money a household needs instead of providing yourself is a problem. The biblical approach is that of giving provision as a representation of yourself, and the difference between the two approaches is profound. But because many men have adopted the first view, and because corporate America dictates the terms under which we may receive a paycheck, we think it is our duty to just go along. But it isn't. A father should bring home the bread, of course. But he should also provide for his family an example for living like a Christian, resisting all attempts of corporate America to press him into its mold (Rom. 12:1–2), seeing Christ in all the clients and customers, and laboring in such a way that would not embarrass him if summoned to do work for a king. For, come to think of it, he *is* working for a King (Col. 3:22).

Questions to Consider:

1. What is the difference between crony capitalism and genuine free market capitalism?
2. Adam Smith wrote of the "invisible hand." How are Christians to understand this?
3. When the Holy Spirit first fills a man in Scripture, what is the result?
4. What is meant by "Christ in the merchant" and "Christ in the customer"?
5. If we decide that our desires are selfish, should we seek to abandon our desires?

Chapter 9

Poverty and Crime at the Head of the Table

Fight Crime, Get Married

We saw earlier that men are going to be "dominant" in every culture. The only real choice we have is whether or not their dominance is going to be constructive or destructive. As Gilder notes, "It is quite impossible to sustain a civilized society if the men are constantly disrupting it."[1] A culture that is not encouraging its men to build is in fact encouraging them to tear down.

The principle that Jesus mentioned concerning Himself applies here as well: he who does not gather, scatters (Luke 11:23). If we do not prevail upon the men to gather, they *will* scatter what others have gathered. "Wise societies provide ample means for young men to affirm themselves without afflicting others."[2] Foolish societies do the opposite, and we have to reckon ourselves as champions in this regard.

Some might think that a man cannot be dominant, specifically in the destructive sense, if he is gone. What if he simply leaves his family for good so that his children never laid eyes on him? But this misses the point entirely. When a man deserts his family like that, his empty chair at the dinner table dominates. It is one of the most significant realities to be found in that home. There are about twenty million kids growing up in single-parent homes today, and overwhelmingly these homes are headed by single moms. If the man is supposed to be there—by God's creation design—and sin means that he is one gone cat, how can this fail to have an enormous impact on those left behind?

There are different ways to calculate that impact, and as we do so we have to remember that the family is an economic institution—the foundational economic institution, in fact. Our word *economics* comes from the Greek word for household—*oikos*—and this is entirely fitting. So this means that when we are looking at the economic costs of the disintegrating modern family, we are not being calloused or mercenary. One of the things a household is supposed to do is perform certain basic economic functions. We don't accuse a doctor when he points out that a heart is not pumping blood the way it ought to. A heart ought to pump blood, and a family ought not to spiral into poverty because dad caught a plane.

Of course, there are many other costs that accrue when families fall apart—spiritual, emotional, and so on—but these are addressed in detail elsewhere in this book. We should not be overly pious and leave the finances out of it. Money translates into meals for kids (or not), and it takes money to buy a winter coat for a toddler. Money is just a way of counting or measuring some essential functions.

Most of us know the sort of thing we are dealing with even apart from sociological studies. We know instinctively that a family with just one parent is going to limp along in many ways. Children from such homes are more likely to drop out of school, more likely to run into trouble with the law, more likely to wind up as single moms themselves, and so on.

Life without parole at the age of twenty-one means that *somebody* is going to pay for that room and board for the next six decades. At any given moment, there are approximately 2.3 million adults in prison. Somebody is paying for all that. Over 700 adults out of every 100,000 are incarcerated. Subtract the 700 from the 100,000 and the resultant sum will identify who is paying for it. And when a father deserts his family, it means that his children are running a much greater risk of winding up in that 700.

We know from the book of Romans that the wages of sin is death (Rom. 6:23), but it turns out that the wages of sin are pretty grim in the meantime also. The wages of sin have a big payout at the end, but there is a *per diem* rate also. God is not mocked. We cannot plant thistles and reap barley (Gal. 6:7).

When it comes to crime, Benjamin Scafidi has cited a study by Harper and McLanahan. The facts are pretty stark. "Boys reared in single-mother households and cohabitating (or 'living together') households are typically more than twice as likely to commit a crime that leads to incarceration, when compared to children who grow up with both their parents."[3]

But there are many more issues other than just the increased likelihood of crime. When you leave your kids, you increase the risks for a lot of additional problems.

> The potential risks to children raised in fragmented families that have been identified in the literature include poverty, mental illness, physical illness, infant mortality, lower educational attainment (including greater risk of dropping out of high school), juvenile delinquency, conduct disorders, adult criminality, and early unwed parenthood.[4]

Then there is also the cost to society at large. In short, pretty much everybody pays.

> Based on the methodology, we estimate that family fragmentation costs U.S. taxpayers *at least $112 billion each and every year,* or more than one trillion each decade.[5]

This is a conservative or minimal estimate.

We have a tendency to veer off after "sexy" theories about the origins of some of our social problems. A recent example would be the thoroughly discredited theory that vaccines are responsible for autism.[6] The kind of alarm that such views generate is an alarm that many in our society find quite congenial, like when somebody says that cell phones cause brain cancer. A certain thrill goes through us . . . it *fits.* But if there is a possibility that autism may be related to the lack of bonding between mother and child, suppose I were to ask for a well-funded study that inquired into whether or not rates of autism increase with the early use of day-care centers for young children, particularly for boys. About the only result I would get from such a request would probably be me having to get an unlisted phone number. To even consider that as a reasonable question to be asked is teetering on the edges of something that feels a lot like repentance.

But common sense responses to issues like this are frequently borne out by the data. A recent study by EMSI, conducted for this book, noted that there are direct economic costs that are borne by the children themselves throughout the course of their lives. Taken in the aggregate, we can say that the lifetime earnings of someone who grew up in a single-parent home will be almost a quarter million dollars less than someone who grew up in a home with both parents. This translates to an economic impact for the nation of $60 billion annually, both through lost wages and the impact of those wages when spent.[7]

> *Where there is no prophetic vision the people cast off restraint, but blessed is he who keeps the law. (Prov. 29:18)*

Because we have refused to listen to what God says, we have "cast off restraint." The way that we heed the prophetic vision is by keeping the law. This means no adultery, no dishonoring of father and mother, and no other acts that disrupt the basic building blocks of society. A failure of father and mother to keep their vows, a failure to make it work, is a real failure, one that translates a great deal of misfortune for others. It is not a "personal choice."

Made to Work

In many inner cities across America, the state has obtained what it *thought* it wanted, and is now the "father"—or perhaps we should say "godfather"—of that system. The problem is that, because it is not being run in accordance with God's design, it cannot work. The state is an *incompetent* father, and the children of the state have spiraled completely out of control. The results of this great social experiment are not just a failure; they are a disaster. It is not as though we no longer know what a fatherless society looks like. We *do* know.

It looks like a crime-riddled society. Superficial observers like to correlate crime and poverty with ethnicity and race. But the real correlation has to be with singleness and sex, specifically unmarried males."[8]

Correlations can, of course, be used in ways that are misleading. We can sometimes jump to hasty conclusions and assert causation where we have no basis for asserting it. But at some point the correlations start to add up to something meaningful. This is reinforced when we think that the statistical correlations are telling us what we all knew already. When you mess your kids up, it messes them up, and father hunger is a great social problem. It is not just a personal problem—it is a culture-wide problem.

In a perverse sort of way, a life of crime often supplies the missing "father needs" better than a distant and bureaucratic government can. A gang leader is close by and personal. A gang leader can be admired by a young buck in ways that an assistant department head for paper shuffling will never be.[9]

We discuss in a later chapter the conflicted nature of the feminist. She wants men to lead while simultaneously not wanting them to. Undisciplined men have a similar internal conflict going themselves. Masculinity thrives on the right kind of discipline, but masculinity also kicks at it. Masculinity thrives on the right kind of work, but it also loves to be lazy. When a culture has undergone a massive failure of nerve, it fails to *insist* when the young men kick against the standards imposed. We don't know what to do with the seething masculinity in the streets because we have lost our masculinity in the places of authority.

This is why a young man who is nothing but disruptive in school, fighting against rules that the school tries to apply to him (somewhat timidly), will shock everybody after graduation by joining the Marine Corps and thriving in boot camp. Nobody thought that what he had been angling for all along was some *real* discipline. Nobody would have guessed, and the failure here was not the young man's.

Theodore Dalrymple points out that there are many men who want to be irresponsible.

> It is a mistake to suppose that all men . . . want to be free. On the contrary, if freedom entails responsibility, many of them want none of it. . . . The aim of untold millions is to be free to do exactly as they choose and for someone else to pay when things go wrong.[10]

But this is just one half of the story. A lot of these men want to be irresponsible in this way because our society thought it would be a good idea to *pay* them for being that way, and remember the earlier lesson: you get more of what you subsidize. So this trick of slumping into irresponsibility only works if there are enough saps running the establishment to let it work. What happens when all the pent-up energy found in young men is *not* harnessed? What happens when it is not disciplined? The problem here is to be located in our cultural leaders who do not have what it takes. Suppose we saw a fine bucking bronco in the stall, but no cowboys signed up for the rodeo. The problem here would be cowboy cowardice, not that the bronco was not up to the task.

The masculine nature, the kind that veers into crime and other patterns of socially destructive behavior, is a masculine nature that will not be tamed by cowards. I was once speaking with a man who had been ministering in Africa, and he had a friendly relationship with the first lady of an African nation. He once asked if there was anything she wanted him to bring over from the United States, and what she asked for really surprised him. She asked for videos of *The Waltons*. The Waltons! Why? The answer was because in those videos the men work. The great social problem she was dealing with was that the men drank and fought while the women worked. Men are built for a fight.[11] They are built for conflict. They are built for discipline. They were created to overcome the dragon.[12] They are built for hard work. But if somebody tries to make them work, they will find out that it is a lot of work. If someone gets in there to train them to fight, they will have a fight on their hands. It is necessary to persevere. Everything depends on it.

When we persevere, the rewards are significant. As Richard Phillips observes, "Probably every man has tasted at some time the deep satisfaction of a job well done. Why does labor have this inherent value? *Because we were made for it.*"[13]

But at the same time, the fallen masculine nature insists that we back away from what we were made for. We were made to till the ground, but God cursed that ground. There are weeds now. The sun is too hot. There is a lion in the streets (Prov. 22:13). I twisted my ankle. Can I go to the bathroom?

Man was also made to be a provider and a protector of the woman. She is not to provide for him; it goes the other way. She should have protection *by* him; she shouldn't need it *from* him. But to take this kind of responsibility on—responsibility for a woman and her children—is to take on a lifetime of sacrifice and hard work. A man who takes a woman to the altar is going there to die to himself. But that is all right because it is not good for man to be alone.

Find Out What Her Name Is and Propose

There is an unfortunate tendency among Christian men to postpone the age of marriage in just the same ways and in the same degree that the world around us has been doing. Men used to marry regularly at around age twenty-three, and now it is closer to twenty-eight. But when God said that it was "not good" that man be alone, when He said that man needed a helper suitable to him, it is likely that He did not intend to meet that need with an empty pizza box. "And behold, among the empty pizza boxes there was not a helper suitable unto him."[14] My father is fond of telling young men that if they are twenty-seven and unmarried, they need to go find out her name and ask her now.[15] Perhaps someone will respond with an appeal to the chimerical gift of "singleness." The apostle Paul had the gift of *celibacy*, which is quite a different thing. The gift of celibacy is not a gift possessed by a twenty-nine-year-old living in his mother's basement, looking at porn. A single man involved in frontier missions, who does not struggle with sexual temptation, has the gift of celibacy. A man with two Xboxes and a trophy from the regional Halo tournament does not.

But men will not take up the masculine responsibilities that a woman brings unless God raises up *leaders* for these men, leaders who will get up in their grill about it. Many men who are wasting their time, and their lives, and their opportunities, know that they are not being very responsible. But they are masculine enough not to be led into leadership by a woman, or by a slight *tsk-tsking* from men who are barely more masculine than they are.

The responsibility of marriage can be very attractive to the masculine mind. But if that responsibility is denied or disrespected, then this turns masculine men into enemies of families in particular and society in general.[16]

Because of our compromises with individualism, and because we use the word *discrimination* like a scarecrow, we tend to dislike generalizations. But Jesus generalized about the Pharisees, and Paul did the same thing with the Cretans. That being the case, "here goes" with regard to the young men. Taking one thing with another, there is no way to lead men away from poverty, away from crime, away from self-destructive habits, away from a life of laziness, without leading them *to a woman*. A woman is not the reward for being responsible. Almost all men need to marry *before* they are entirely responsible adults. A suitor should be a reasonable candidate for future responsibility, but he needs a woman to get there. In this world, a woman is God's chief instrument for *making* a man responsible. He uses her to *get* him there. Just as the fear of the Lord is the beginning of knowledge, so also is the love of a good woman the beginning of male responsibility. Humanly speaking, you cannot get much masculinity without femininity.

These ideas about singleness, tragically, have gotten entrenched as something of an evangelical tradition. This is one of those places where we have to turn away from what we have inherited from our fathers. But we should do it the same way the Reformers did, with the same kind of balance.

> Although the Reformation did come to extol the patriarchal family, its initial success lay in persuading a generation to abandon the faith of its fathers. Ezekiel 20:18 became a banner for Protestant reformers: "Do not walk in the statutes of your fathers, nor observe their ordinances, nor defile yourselves with their idols."[17]

The idol is singleness. The idol is personal freedom, and in the name of Jesus. And just as men generally are not thriving, so our evangelical men are not thriving. And why? We are trying to will-power our way into good when God has already said "not good." I would suggest that we try putting the fish back in the tank.

We forget that God uses means. We are too often gnostic or hyperrationalist in our assumptions about "inner spirituality." We have come to think that a bath is a reward for having gotten clean already. We think that food is the reward for having grown big and strong. We think that sexual pleasure with a woman is a reward for having proven over many years that you don't need a woman at all. We are like the fellow at the bank, discovering that he can only borrow money if he proves to them that he doesn't really need it.

If a father sees this problem I am talking about, and his boys are still relatively young, what should he do? He can prepare his son to be a godly husband for a woman, but it will take the woman to complete the task.

Young boys are in touch with their passions, be it hunger for food, competition, bursts of anger, or something else.

When a boy is young, his unbridled passions are relatively harmless. *So what if he pitched a fit in the cereal aisle at the grocery store?* we might think. *The world didn't end.* Or maybe it's no big deal to you that he threw his baseball glove at the first baseman for missing an easy grounder. The temptation is to indulge such foibles, treating them as not much. Then, when the boy gets older, and is capable of doing real damage, his parents panic. He now has a driver's license, and the way he is driving could lead to somebody getting killed. He is old enough to get somebody pregnant, and some of the girls at the skate park are looking at him like they think that would be fun. And so when his parents panic, they clamp down with a bunch of rules. Of course, a boy who has been almost entirely undisciplined for fifteen years is not going to take to *that* very well, and so it sets the stage for more conflict.

It really ought to go the other way. A young boy who is being prepared for manhood should be taught the ropes of self-control when he is young, and when his passions are the same size that he is. When he scrapes his knee, his father should hold him for a minute, then teach him to "blow it out." When he loses a close game that he wanted to win very badly, his father should teach him good sportsmanship. When he is petulant because his mother won't let him have a bag of chips half an hour before dinner, his father should joke with him about it and make sure he cheers right up. In all this, the father is doing something very important, which is keeping his son out of the penitentiary (Prov. 23:14).

The external discipline that a father brings his son should be considerable when the son is young, and it should be gradually lifted over time. By the time the son leaves home (as he should, and as he should *want* to do), he needs to have been prepared for the complete liberty that he will soon have. He is not being prepared for autonomy (or for "singleness"), but rather for marriage. What a young man needs at one stage of his life is godly preparation for what he needs at the next stage of his life. "A wise parent understands that his government is to be crowned by an act of emancipation; and it is a great problem, to accomplish that emancipation gracefully."[18]

And of course, we should include a few words of encouragement for those men who are reading this ten years after it would have done them a lot more good. The thing to remember is that the principles don't change, the Holy Spirit is still at work among His people, and, as my father used to say, God picks us up where we are, and not where we should have been.

Questions to Consider:

1. Why does it take courage to discipline and teach young men?
2. Why is it foolhardy for a young man to postpone marriage so he can work on his porn problem?
3. In what way is femininity necessary to masculinity?
4. Why must the passions of boys be addressed when they are young?
5. What can be done when a man is already grown?

Chapter 10

Church Fathers, Ha

Fathers for the Church

One of the fundamental qualifications given for church leadership in the New Testament is that we must have men who know *what it means to be a father.* If we continue to ignore the obvious, it gets pretty complicated. Because we don't understand how imitation governs the world, we have neglected one of the fundamental realities that we are supposed to imitate. As a result, everything downstream from that goes all to pieces also. Consider Paul's words to Timothy:

> He must manage his own household well, with all dignity keeping his children submissive, for if someone does not know how to manage his own household, how will he care for God's church? (1 Tim. 3:4–5)

Paul has extended grace, mercy, and peace from God our *Father* (1 Tim. 1:2). God is the Father of Jesus Christ, and is therefore, in a manner of speaking, the Father-in-law of the Christian church.

The Christian church is the bride of Christ. Within this church, spiritual leaders are "fathers" to their congregations. One of the central qualifications for a father in a congregation is that he be able to demonstrate for the people what a godly, effective father can do in the home. Instead of this, we have decided to substitute three years of graduate study. The results we have gotten should not have been a surprise to us.

Some Protestants object to this line of thought because of the abuses that have occurred in church history related to this. Jesus prohibited calling any man "father," didn't He?

> But you are not to be called rabbi, for you have one teacher, and you are all brothers. And call no man your father on earth, for you have one Father, who is in heaven. Neither be called instructors, for you have one instructor, the Christ. The greatest among you shall be your servant. Whoever exalts himself will be humbled, and whoever humbles himself will be exalted. (Matt. 23:8–12)

There are three honorific terms we are told not to use in a certain way (in a way that obscures the Fatherhood of God). Those terms are teacher, father, and instructor. Protestants object to the use of phrases like father, padre, or pope, but we have teachers and instructors galore. When it comes to Bible *teachers*, Christ's words here don't even slow us down. There is an abuse here that Jesus requires us to reject, but we must not try to obey Him through a superstitious reaction to certain words. We must reject the error He was talking about. We must not have teachers, fathers, or instructors as *mediators*. We are all brothers, and we all have a Father in Heaven, and we are all instructed by Christ.

With this warning in mind, *if* we keep it in mind, we do have fathers in the faith. Paul speaks this way very plainly.

> For though you have countless guides in Christ, you do not have many fathers. For I became your father in Christ Jesus through the gospel. I urge you, then, be imitators of me. (1 Cor. 4:15–16)

The reason we need fathers in the church is because there are lessons that cannot be learned unless we learn them by imitation. Children imitate, and when we learn by imitation, the lessons go deeper than when we learn them in any other way. Christians are to imitate God, as dearly loved children (Eph. 5:1). In the Corinthian passage, in the next verse, Paul told them that this is why he had sent Timothy to them—he was a dearly loved child, and he could remind them of Paul's way of life (v. 17). We can learn from our spiritual fathers at a distance—from other children of theirs, or from accounts of their lives.

Churches need *fathers* to govern them, but unfortunately, today's church appears to show all the signs of being managed by the ecclesiastical equivalent of single moms. Paul requires that the church be governed *by road-tested fathers*. Do their children mind them? Do they conduct well the household management tasks that fathers are called to undertake? If they don't know how to be a father in a home, then what on earth makes us think that they could perform the necessary task of being a father in the church? This plainly illustrates what Paul is after—he is seeking fathers for the church.

This also explains why the controversy over women's ordination is not going to go away very soon. Because we have neglected this crucial testing ground and gone for the graduate student test instead, we have not surprisingly drifted. Once the drift sets in, it is not possible to arbitrarily stop that drift.[1] For several centuries we have exalted some very feminine virtues to the highest place in the church and have demanded that the men conform to those standards. Unfortunately, if *those* are the standards, women would do a better job at being women pastors than men do at being women pastors. If we must have women pastors, women would be better at it, or so it would seem.

But evangelicals are still stuck with Paul's inscrutable (to us) prohibition in 1 Timothy 2:11–15.[2] It is not a coincidence, incidentally, that the requirement that bishops be tested family men, fathers who rule their households well, is a requirement that immediately follows this prohibition of women in ministry. We should recall that in the original letter to Timothy, there were no chapter breaks. And yet, because we have neglected the qualification that he must be a "reliable father," we have patched together some other characteristics that we think would be "nice." Thus we have come to demand essentially feminine virtues of our ministers but are stuck with this arbitrary line from the Bible that disqualifies the most qualified members of the church—as far as being sweet goes. This creates a demand among evangelicals for some exegetical ingenuity.[3]

The Shack and Father Hunger

Because of all this, the church is afflicted with a desperate case of father hunger. And as with other forms of hunger, past a certain point, appeals to reason aren't going to cut it. If you get to that point, everybody is going to do what everybody is going to do. This is what explains a phenomenon like *The Shack*, a best-selling book by William Young.[4] In this book, the protagonist is named Mack, and a few years before the book opens, his youngest daughter named Missy had been kidnapped and presumably murdered. He himself had had a terrible childhood, and had finally run away from home as a teenager after poisoning his father. One day Mack receives a mysterious note from "Papa," his wife's favorite name for God, inviting him to come meet at the shack where his daughter had likely been killed. He decides to go, and after he gets there, the shack is transformed, and he finds himself on a weekend retreat with all three persons of the Trinity. Over the course of that weekend, he learns all kinds of things about himself and about the world that he had never suspected. That, in sum, is the basic setup.

William Young, the author, knows with a profound clarity that fatherlessness is the rot that is eating away at the modern soul. The clear appeal of the book is because of the ache created by fatherlessness, which, when coupled with the metaphoric solutions offered, explains the popularity of the book. So in a book clearly written to deal with the pain of fatherlessness, how does Young go about it? He makes God the Father, "Papa," a large, beaming African American *woman*.[5] The Holy Spirit is a shimmery Asian woman named Sarayu, mysterious and "way out there." Jesus is simply Jesus, and is masculine after a kind, but in that unique way possessed by camp counselors and youth ministers with muscular forearms. And here is a taste of the down-home weekend retreat-like relationship that is going to fix Mack.

> Mack followed her soft humming down a short hallway and into an open kitchen-dining area, complete with a small four-seat table and wicker-backed chairs. The inside of the cabin was roomier than he had expected. Papa was working on something with her back to him, flour flying as she swayed to the music of whatever she was listening to. The song obviously came to an end, marked by a couple of last shoulder and hip shakes. Turning to face him, she took off the earphones.[6]

Meet God the Father Almighty, maker of Heaven and earth. Young is by no means a dunce—he is very clear that this is just an appearance, an accommodation. But the image, the metaphor, the feel of this whole book, is warm and maternal, cozy and nonthreatening. The center of the discussions is the kitchen. The need is a deep father hunger, but this is not met by a *father,* but by the enveloping warmth of a comfort mama who makes a lot of comfort food. This symbolism is not incidental to the message of the book. It *is* the central message of the book. You need a father? Here, talk to your mother about it.

And this reveals the bedrock problem with the whole thing. There is no way we can hide from ourselves that we have a need for a father—it has gotten that obvious—but we cannot bring ourselves to *repent* and have our hearts turned back to actual fathers. We cannot bring ourselves to honor our (admittedly sinful) fathers so that our lives might go well for us in the land that God gave to us. This means that we are stuck. We know the problem is fatherlessness, but we have no intention of honoring our real fathers the way they should be honored. This is because the sin of fatherlessness is one that is shared by both fathers and children. And repentance, we should remember, when it is given, will be bestowed on *both* sides of the generational divide.

> Behold, I will send you Elijah the prophet before the great and awesome day of the LORD comes. And he will turn the hearts of fathers to their children *and the hearts of children to their fathers,* lest I come and strike the land with a decree of utter destruction. (Mal. 4:5–6)

This generation of evangelicals really is fatherless and adrift. They know that, they ache over it, they cannot pretend not to know it, but they have no intention of turning back to their fathers, at least not yet. And that means repentance has not yet been given. And before we turn back in repentance, we will try any number of other expedients. Ironically, this is what is happening in the debate over the ordination of women. Why do so many want to ordain mothers? Because they need a father who will say no.

Bodies Matter

The same problem is illustrated and revealed in a different way in James K. A. Smith's book *Desiring the Kingdom.*[7] Parts of this book are outstanding, but the parts that carry this malady of our age really undo the benefit. The main failing of the book was that while Smith had some good punches, he managed to pull them all. He had some nice moves, but it was shadow boxing (1 Cor. 9:26). In other words, he doesn't really want anyone to actually *embody* what he is arguing for, which is odd because he is arguing for a worship that shapes our desires and results in a robust and *embodied* life.

Initially his thesis seems great. Worship shapes desire, and we should measure our success in the church and in the academy by how well we do in forming particular kinds of people—people who love Christ and one another. Education is about formation, not information. All this is great. We have bodies, given to us by God, and our bodies matter. What we do with those bodies matters. It matters a lot. And that is what Smith is arguing for here. Our bodies matter a great deal.

It would seem that there would be a great deal of common ground here. I pray for this regularly—that worship would become and remain central for us. I pray that we would worship God rightly, and that the water of life would flow over the threshold of Ezekiel's temple, getting deeper and deeper as it goes, until it inundates the whole world. I pray that our worship would be central, and that it would shape everything we do—in business, in the arts, in education, in medicine, and so on. Worship, rightly offered, changes us and transforms the world. Smith seems to be saying this, but he isn't really. And not surprisingly, this issue of fatherlessness lies right at the root. Smith writes,

> Worship, like creation, ends as it began: with God's blessing. The minister raises her hands, we stretch out ours to receive, and God's blessing is proclaimed.[8]

Her hands? What is wrong with this? Why is it not permissible for a woman to raise her hands to give a ministerial blessing? As we know, Paul forbids it (1 Tim. 2:12). But why? It is not because Paul believes women to be incapable of the requisite knowledge, or that he thinks women cannot exhibit the necessary godly character. No, the reason is her body. Women can't be ministers because they are women. Women have breasts and wombs, and the presence of breasts and wombs matter. Women were embodied with a different calling than was assigned to men when they were given *their* bodies. Bodies matter. I do not want anyone to mistake me here. I can understand someone differing with me on the ordination of women. But for those urging this novelty, I would rather not hear from them about bodies not mattering in the name of bodies mattering.

Let's be frank. If sermon *content* were the only thing that mattered, I can think of quite a few unordained women whom I would rather listen to than quite a few ordained men. But the content is not the issue. Here is a place where conservatives know that bodies matter, and liberals want to focus on ethereal ideas, floating above the congregation. It is apparent that here is a place where Smith is actually abandoning his case. He cannot spend a book arguing that embodiment is the thing, and that bodies matter, and then, when we reject women as ministers because they have women's bodies (proving that they are in fact women), say that we are obsessing about bodies.

Bodies matter in the faithful obedience of men and women. Bodies also matter when we sin with them (Rom. 6:12). We are to present our bodies as a living sacrifice (Rom. 12:1–2). This is why conservative believers have been so adamant about issues like abortion (which is the destruction of one body, the desecration of another, and the defilement of a third) and homosexual ordination and marriage. Bodies really do matter. Sex matters. But here is Smith:

> I don't mean to communicate an alarmist fear of culture in the spirit of the "culture wars" (which, by the way, I think are often tilting at windmills rather than targeting the real, substantive threats to Christian discipleship—fixated on gay marriage but eagerly affirming capitalism).[9]

Get that? Gay marriage is not a substantive threat to Christian discipleship, but building a business is. And note that opposition to gay marriage is represented as an alarmist fear "of culture," instead of what it is—a dedicated opposition to the degradation of culture. When some performance artist wants to spray-paint a priceless painting at the National Gallery and the security guard tackles him, he does not do so because he has an "alarmist fear of culture." The guard is *defending* culture, not attacking it.

In short, Smith wants worship to shape and form folks, but if the formation he has in view involves disparagement of free markets, accepting the Word preached from feminine mouths and the sacraments from feminine hands, and sniffing at believing efforts to beat back the sodomification of America, then whatever kind of worship service he wants, we should not want it. If that is what is cooking, why should we want to eat?

> And yet the integration of a worship practice that is economic, tethered to the wider scope of Scripture, functions as a kind of haunting reminder of an economics that refuses the assumption of the capitalist imagination.[10]

If he meant resistance to crony crapitalism, which we addressed earlier, then of course *amen*. But from a number of comments made throughout the book, I have surmised that is not what he is talking about. He is talking about getting rid of free markets—the kind of markets the Holy Spirit loves to create.

He wants to substitute coercive markets for free markets, and he wants worship services that will form the kind of people who would go for that. But biblical worship will form men who always hate such statist coercion.

Then there is an odd, twisty-turn. First, he says this: "Intentional Christian worship that includes the elements we've described above, and that draws upon a holistic tradition of worship that activates the whole body, is packed with formative power."[11] Formative, yes, but not *too* formative. Notice what he says next: "Such a monastic abstention for cultural labor sees itself as engaged in a struggle, but it forswears any pretension to a 'culture war' because it doesn't think it's the job of the church to transform the world."[12]

What? Engage with the world, but make sure you don't change anything?[13] This is what I meant by pulling the punches. This is not the kind of worship that will ever produce a prophet who is any kind of handful for the authorities. John the Baptist got arrested, not for challenging the norms of economic justice, but rather for talking about Herod's sex life. But if the ancient schools of the prophets had followed this pattern, the results would have been pretty thin. The prophets in Elisha's school would have had to spend a lot of evenings in their cave doing amateur renditions of *Penzance*. "We go, we go, we go!" "But you don't go!"

Notice how this absolutely gags the possibility of the church having a prophetic voice. We are resolved to speak truth to power, but we let said powers know (through back channels) that we are just making noise to keep our base happy. We have absolutely no intention of actually changing anything. If we had *that* kind of intention, the powers that be might actually fight back. And if they fought back, somebody on our side might get hurt. Here is the bottom line: Smith is right about the centrality of worship. But if it is "triumphalist" to want to change the world, why should we care about changing our worship at all? We have anemic worship *now*.

We are successful at not changing anything now. Why go through a lot of fuss and bother to develop a form of worship that will *also* not change anything?

Real Fathers in the Church

And so we now can return to the top. We need fathers in the church. We need authority. We need some John Knox beards. We need shepherds, the kind who, like David, can handle the occasional bear or lion. Real ministers really do need to be tough, and we need to remember that the reputation of ministerial milquetoastery—of ministers as the third sex—is not really all *that* unfair. Generations of "the nicest young man in the church" have been urged by the church ladies to consider the ministry, and because it was a vocation that by common consent involved no bleeding knuckles and lots of being nice to people, over time the church has come to consider the best candidate for future ministry to be "that sweet boy."

We are all aware of the type—from real life and from literature. The literary portrayals are sometimes overstated and are unfair for that reason, but they still work, and they work for a reason. That reason is that the caricatures answer to something that most of us have seen in real life. From the psalm-singer David Gamut in Cooper's stories, to the Rev. Mr. Kinosling in the Penrod stories, to Mr. Collins in *Pride and Prejudice*, we who are ministers have the opportunity to see ourselves *as the world sees us*. We ought to think about it more than we usually do. In your average Western, when the work of fighting the Indians warms up, "the parson" is usually underfoot and useless.

So here is the deal. When a man puts on a clerical collar, he needs to know that a certain masculine gravity is necessary to keep that collar from pulling him (by association and connotation) in a direction he shouldn't really want to go. If he has that gravity, and is aware of the long connotations associated with clericalism (and is familiar with the resultant anticlericalism), I think that wearing a robe while preaching, or wearing a collar, could be entirely a good thing. But unless he thinks it through, others are going to imitate him without much thought, and some of those who imitate him are going to be mousy little men *already* standing chest deep in the pond of effeminacy. And when they put on the collar, it will just plain pull them under. They already exhibit the tendencies that created the caricature in the first place—they are the nice boy who went to seminary as instructed by the church ladies—and then they adopt a uniform that has a lot of these standing connotations for the surrounding world to tag him with. I was watching a very nice "reverend" being interviewed on television one time, and he was *so* gentle and did everything but pat the viewers on the back of the hand. It was obvious, and his collar made it screamingly obvious.

I know that some readers will have been blessed with *no* experience of what I am talking about at all, and it will seem to them that I am therefore talking nonsense. I am glad for them. They grew up with a gruff and collared Lutheran pastor who was a Navy Seal before going to seminary, a man who kept a spittoon in the vestry, and so the natural conclusion they might draw is that Wilson is being hypersensitive here. So sensitive, in fact, that we suspect a little effeminacy, do we not?

But our problem with centuries of an effeminate ministry is not yet widely recognized, even though it is a deeply rooted problem in the culture of the West. I have a very high view of the ministerial calling, and believe it to be a scriptural one, but I also believe that a certain kind of clericalism was largely responsible for the rise of a virulent anticlericalism. Before we head back there again, could we talk a bit about what we did wrong last time?

Questions to Consider:

1. In what way is it biblical to think of a minister as a father?
2. How should these fathers in the church be "road-tested" fathers?
3. If effeminacy in valued in the ministry, why will we have a hard time keeping women out of the ministry?
4. In what way is *The Shack* indicative of a deep-seated father hunger?
5. When it comes to women's ordination, why should we say that "bodies matter"?

Chapter 11

Conflicted Feminism

The Nature of the World

The doctrine of *creation* is very important. If we are the end product of so many millions of years of evolution, there is no reason to take anything as a fixed given. The views of women are in evolutionary flux, just like everything else. The evolutionary faith holds that hydrogen can, given enough heat and time, turn into armadillos, dwarf stars, cinnamon sticks for your ice cream, and Senator Al Franken, Democrat from Minnesota. Put more simply, anything whatsoever can morph into anything else.

This makes sense as one of the basic logical options, if you think about it. Either somebody put the universe here, or somebody didn't. If somebody didn't, then there has to be a way to account for the astounding variations we see around us on every hand. If matter is eternal, then matter *has* to be able to morph. Darwin didn't come up with this as one of the basic options—the basic pagan outlook has always gravitated to it. Ovid, at the very beginning of *The Metamorphoses,* says that maybe God made the world. Or maybe there was Chaos and one day the gods popped out. *Something* is eternal—either the Creator or all this stuff. All Darwin did is give the denial of the need for a Creator a bright cherry red wax job, after which his disciples at *National Geographic* shined it up real nice.

But notice what this does to sexuality, and that it *does* do something to sexuality. All kinds of critters around the world have morphed themselves into a number of interesting options in this regard. There are asexual reproducers, like your basic bacteria. There are hermaphroditic animals, like your pulmonate snails. There are the regular old guy and gal species, like Fido and Fifi, and so it seems there is no reason why we couldn't grow ourselves a third or fourth sex. Let the experimentation begin! Let a thousand flowers bloom. But this only makes sense in a blind and accidental world—not in an engineered one. If intelligent design is true, then there might be design, and we might have to use our intelligence.

If the world is *created*, then it becomes necessary to follow the manufacturer's instructions—which goes a long way in explaining why a number of people would find the existence of a Creator God more than a little inconvenient. If we start messing around with this equipment as though there were no factory of origin, but there actually is a factory of origin, there is a better than even chance that we are going to get all our warranties voided.

So the debate over creation is not a debate being conducted by disinterested scholars in a glorious vacuum of scientific disinterestedness and objectivity. It is not as though the issue of evolution has no practical or ethical ramifications. We are discussing whether or not a Creator God engineered everything we see around us, whether He left an operations manual with us to use, and whether or not He will conduct an inventory and audit when we are all done with it. The way some people are using the equipment, we do not find it surprising that they stridently insist that the idea of an audit is a myth that comes down to us from Neanderthal times.

But think of it this way. When Adam strolled through the garden and picked and peeled the first orange—and what a lot of fun *that* must have been—and he was holding that peeled orange in the palm of his hand, do you think he had any trouble figuring out how to pull those segments apart in order to eat them one bite at a time? I mean, the instructions are practically written there on the inside peel. I know that Martha Stewart has figured how to get them to do a bunch of other things so that they can float in a punch bowl for a photo shoot, but the basic reality still remains. The creational reality remains. And when Adam and Eve made love for the first time, there was a way for them to figure it out—despite not having any relationship section at a nearby Barnes & Noble. At least, the fact that we are all here means that *somebody* figured it out.

If the world is created, then men are always going to be men and women are always going to be women. But if, despite this, the men and women convince themselves that the world is not created, and that they can strike out on their own (as can the other sex), this bright idea doesn't actually change the way the world is. It just changes what some confused people are saying about it. Abraham Lincoln once asked a man how many legs a sheep would have if we called the tail a leg. Five, came the reply. No, not really, Lincoln said. Calling the tail a leg doesn't make it a leg.

If you combine evolutionary assumptions and postmodern relativism, you get a toxic sexual mix, something I have been calling pomosexuality. The world's sophisticates have come up with five genders (and counting). I was signing up for a new account with an Internet giant the other day, and when it came to indicating my sex, they thoughtfully gave me three options to choose from: male, female, and "other." I won't say which Web site this was, but it rhymes with Foogle. Their motto eschews being evil, but they have allowed themselves some leeway on being confused.

Gender-bending is what comes of living in a world full of fallen and sinful desires coupled with certain evolutionary assumptions that allow one the liberty of trying to evolve into some other interesting sexual identity. This is why we now have gay, lesbian, bisexual, transgendered, and what used to be called normal. We also have riffs on these—queer and metrosexual, for example. This is a complicated process, kind of like getting a new sport added to the Olympic games. Who knows where this endless process of morphing will end up?

But believing yourself to live in an endlessly morphing cosmos does not make this sexual meander possible. For the culture at large, it makes it *necessary*. This is because Scripture lays down an inexorable law: you become like what you worship. This is true of the living God and it is true of idols. Worshippers of the true God become more and more like Him. Worshippers of idols become more and more like those idols.

In Psalm 115, we are told that foolish men make idols that have sightless eyes, deaf ears, dumb mouths, and so forth. Those who make them, the psalmist says, are "like unto them" (KJV). A man comes to resemble what he worships. We see the same principle working in the other direction as well. We are being transformed from one degree to another as we behold the Lord (in worship). This is what the apostle Paul points to when he says that we are being transformed from one degree of glory to another. This is happening because of what we are beholding in worship (2 Cor. 3:18).

This is not a supposition resting in some rickety way on the top of just a couple of verses. G. K. Beale has done a masterful job in demonstrating that this is actually one of the great themes found throughout Scripture.

> God has made humans to reflect him, but if they do not commit themselves to him, they will not reflect him, but something else in creation. At the core of our beings, we are imaging creatures. It is not possible to be neutral on this issue: we either reflect the Creator or something in creation.[1]

If we believe that the ultimate reality is simply evolutionary flux, then that will be our final and ultimate principle. Evolutionary flux has become our god, and we will grow into the likeness of that god, as much as we can. This is the deep religious motivation behind the troubled identity issues that Michael Jackson had—but Jackson is nothing more than a parable for our time. He did not treat his race as a defined boundary. He did not even treat his *face* as a defined boundary. So if *change* is our object of worship, then change is what we will become like.

Sexual choices are not a matter of taste, or of genetics, or of mere cultural custom. Sexual expressions are religious expressions. Peter Jones writes,

> The pagan gospel preaches that redemption is *liberation from* the Creator and *repudiation of* creation's structures. It offers the "liberation" of sex from its heterosexual complementary essence. The Christian gospel proclaims that redemption is *reconciliation with* the Creator and the *honoring of* creation's goodness. This gospel celebrates the goodness of sex within its rightful, heterosexual limits.[2]

Look around the world. In one way it would be easy (too easy) to simply say that standards have slipped and that there are too many weirdoes these days. But this is a phenomenon far too widespread to be a case of standards *slipping*—on the contrary, this is a case of standards *changing*, or, to put it bluntly, it is a changing of the gods.

The Father Who Does Not Change

So coming back to the theme of this book, we should be able to see why the worship of God *the Father* is so important. Without that, we will no longer be able to maintain the understanding of fatherhood that grew and developed during the course of Christendom's rise and maturation. You cannot remove God and demand that we still be able to keep His likeness. Like it or not, we will take on the likeness of the god we replaced Him with. In fact, once we have removed ourselves from the worship of the Father, it is not long before we cannot tolerate even the presence of His likeness in others, if that likeness is the result of their worship, and not mere mimicry.

"In a sort of ghastly simplicity we remove the organ and demand the function," C. S. Lewis famously wrote. "We make men without chests and expect of them virtue and enterprise. We laugh at honour and are shocked to find traitors in our midst. We castrate and bid the geldings be fruitful."[3] This passage is quite familiar to many, but I don't mind citing it again because it is something that all of us really ought to memorize.

To return to the illustration of the orange, and the earlier point that women are more in touch with the creational realities that are resident within their bodies, we can see that women are like those orange segments. And they get readily exasperated with men who deny this, even when they were initially the ones who *told* the men to deny this. In fact, they are exasperated *especially* if they told the men to do this (and they did). "I wish . . . Oh, never mind."

Jesus gives us quite a striking image of two houses, both of which *look* fine. One is built on His words at the foundational level, an asset that is largely invisible from the street. The other has no foundation, a fact hidden from curbside by some cleverly arranged shrubbery. The difference between the two houses is not revealed until the moment of crisis, until the storm (Matt. 7:24–29).

Questions of identity are foundational. This is why debates over our "identity" politics are so divisive and polarizing. Questioning someone's identity just guarantees a defensive reaction. If people get into a debate over whether it is raining outside or not, it is possible that somebody might get a little defensive about it, provided they are a little insecure. But if you are questioning what someone claims to *be*, at the rock-bottom foundational level, the debate will necessarily be fierce. And if you are right in the questions you are asking, you can expect fireworks.

So the culture wars in America are not really about what an American is, but rather about what a human being is. "So God created man in his own image, in the image of God he created him; male and female he created them" (Gen 1:27). Our created nature was thrust upon us—let us speak frankly. We did not volunteer for it. Before we were born, we were not up in Heaven filling out forms. We did not check any boxes requesting to be born "male" or "female." We did not ask for it. It follows from this that we cannot erase it.

Trying to deny what you are is constant, unremitting *work*. It is like trying to hold a fully inflated beach ball underwater. If you do that long enough, your arms start quivering. And if someone questions your assumed identity ("Whatcha got under there?"), what they are doing is poking at your arms—the kind of thing that excites comment.

When women indulge in rape fantasies, we can of course agree that this is demented. It is a corruption, yes, but what is it a corruption *of*? When women want a man to step in and play the role of the dominant male, they can want this in extremely pathological ways. They can read all about their quasi-rape setups—let us call it a ravishing look from Lord Greycastle, who would not be told no—in a paperback bodice buster they bought at the grocery store. And there are plenty more where that one came from. So this also is a corruption of some sort, but what is it a corruption *of*? What is going on?

When this subject is seriously broached, feminists and the society cowed by them want to know if we seriously mean to defend, in this day and age, a *Taming of the Shrew* approach, and they ask the question with lowered eyebrows indicating trouble ahead. "Are you serious?" That is the signal to backpedal, and lots do. But inside more than one feminist, and way more than one feminist-indoctrinated woman, there is an internal, conflicted dialogue that goes something like this: "*Please* don't back off. Please have a spine. What am I saying? Nobody will know. This is so wrong. I don't believe this. I am an educated woman with progressive views. . . . Why do pencil-necks make me so frustrated? Just say that you think *Shrew* is the very best Shakespeare play *ever*, and no, not in the sense of having subversive, ironic, and postmodern layers. *Please*—" Who doesn't like *Kiss Me, Kate!*

Needless to say, many of these conflicted internal dialogues do not have a happy ending. The couple does go out to Starbucks for coffee and a conversation about self-referential irony in Shakespeare, but they go Dutch. Gak. Feminism has demanded the formation of a certain kind of man and, having attained to that, we are discovering that feminists look down on this kind of man as much as everybody else throughout history has.

Male authority is an erotic necessity. In order to make love, a man must be hard and the woman soft. This is not just a physiological detail, but a metaphor for their whole relationship. Feminists, having demanded soft men, have discovered that it is beyond exasperating to be locked in a rape fantasy with some Caspar

Milquetoast. *Ravish me!* she pleads with her eyes. Let's go down to the aquarium, he says, and look at the endangered species exhibit. If you are going to go for soft, then another woman makes better sense. Lesbianism, it turns out, has an internal logic.

We are fortunate that we live in the world God made, as opposed to the world created in the fevered imaginations of our urbanite secularists. These cosmopolitan denizens of blue failed states, containing all the economic prowess of southern Europe, only without castles in the background, want to sneer at the obvious. Because we live in the world made and governed by the goodness of God, we have the luxury of knowing that the obvious can never be outlawed. Seven Congresses in a row couldn't do it, and the president can hand out as many signing pens as he likes, but up is still up and grass is still green. But while the obvious cannot be outlawed, pointing it out *can* be heavily penalized—which is another issue. The emperor is still naked, but the little boy who pointed it out was taken from his parents and is now living under state-supervised foster care.

The Bible does not teach that women as a class are subordinate to men as a class. Each woman is to be subject to her own husband. It has been too infrequently pointed out that this means she is *not* subject to all the others. Still less does the biblical requirement mean that men are superior to women. Now in order to talk about this, I will need to use words like *superior* and *inferior*, which causes the modern egalitarian reader to bridle a bit. All I can do is refer you to the discussion in chapter 2 of egalitarianism, remind you that we are not talking about ultimate worth in the sight of God, and ask you to bear with me for a few paragraphs.

An observant critic of feminism once asked why a first-rate woman would want to become a third-rate man. A first-rate woman needs to be a first-rate woman *to* a first-rate man. It is not possible to take a man of lesser gifts and say that because he is male, he is therefore superior to any given female. The biblical form of patriarchy is not that form which claims superiority of every man over every woman. C. S. Lewis makes this point when he is discussing the humility of Portia over against Bassanio.

> Many women in love, many wives, perhaps many queens, have at some time said or thought as much. Portia wished that for Bassanio's sake, she might be trebled "twenty times herself. A thousand times more fair, ten thousand times more rich," and protests that, as things are, "the full sum of her is sum of nothing," "an unlesson'd girl." It is prettily said and sincerely said. But I should feel sorry for the common man, such as myself, who was led by this speech into the egregious mistake of walking into Belmont and behaving as though Portia really *were* an unlessoned girl. A man's forehead reddens to think of it. She may speak thus to Bassanio: but *we* had better remember that we are dealing with a great lady.[4]

It is not as though we have two horizontal lines, with the upper one consisting of men and the lower one of women. Rather, we have two vertical lines, side by side, one of men and the other of women. The male line extends slightly above the female line, such that any woman, however gifted, is in a good position to find a man she can respect and look up to. But obviously, a woman of superior attainments is superior to most of the males in the other line. Queen Esther, advisor to the emperor, precisely because of her submission to her husband, was in a place of far greater influence than virtually all of the men in Susa. Imagine a Christian president with a godly wife, and both of them understand the Pauline teaching of headship and submission in marriage. She will have more authority than most men have ever dreamed of having.

Wherever the human race walks, we pull the bell curve after us. And we are constituted male and female at every point along that curve.

Here is another illustration. Imagine any mechanism that requires two parts—bell and clapper, say. Big Ben in London has both components, as does a five-dollar bell you buy at a yard sale. But it would be a stretch to say the bell portion of the yard-sale bell was superior to the clapper in Big Ben. That kind of comparison, that kind of thinking, makes no sense. A biblical view of women does not prohibit women from great achievements consistent with her nature. But when women adopt an unbiblical view of themselves, they cannot understand God rightly. If they will not love and worship the Father, they cannot understand themselves, or what they are supposed to be doing. This puts them in a state of continual exasperation with the very men who refuse to contradict them.

In short, feminists are women, and this means they do not get to opt out of the curse that God placed on the relationship between the sexes. After the fall, God told Eve that her desire would be for her husband. To the woman he said, "I will surely multiply your pain in childbearing; in pain you shall bring forth children. Your desire shall be for your husband, and he shall rule over you" (Gen. 3:16). The only other time this particular phrase is used in the Bible is in the very next chapter in the warning God gives to Cain, and the similarity in usage is quite striking. "If you do well, will you not be accepted? And if you do not do well, sin is crouching at the door. Its desire is for you, but you must rule over it" (Gen. 4:7). The desire in both cases is a desire for mastery, and the "rule" in both cases is defensive retaliation.

At the same time, the woman is conflicted about her desire for mastery, and hopes on another level that she will *not* get her way. This is because, prior to the fall, God had created her to be a help. Speaking of the Hebrew word for helper, *kenegdo*, Rick Phillips says this: "The idea is that the woman corresponds to the man, not as a mirror image but as a puzzle piece that clicks."[5] The curse makes women want to lead their husbands, but when their husbands abdicate and let them do this, they don't like that either.[6] This is a curse-based tendency, not a deterministic thing. It explains our temptations but does not require us to sin in this way.

For many years I have used the illustration of how differently oriented the sexes are to each other by pointing to a novel written by a man for men, as opposed to a novel written by a woman for women.[7] In the book for men, the plot is all about the mission—getting the gold back, or finding the cattle, or winning the battle, or saving the world. When a woman enters the action, her role is to help (with the cattle, gold, whatever). He is mission oriented. The book for women has a different plot structure. In this book, the relationship *is* the plot. First they like each other *kinda,* and then something happens to threaten the relationship, and then they like each other again, *only more now.* She is relationship oriented.

But what happens when this goes to seed? There is clearly a God-given orientation here to begin with. "For man was not made from woman, but woman from man. Neither was man created for woman, but woman for man" (1 Cor. 11:8–9). At the same time, the account in Genesis shows us that these basic orientations have been cursed. Sin affects them. What happens when the curse is not countered with grace? Rick Phillips makes a shrewd observation:

> God's curse on the man draws him unwholesomely *away* from the woman, even as God's curse on the woman draws her unwholesomely *toward* the man . . . God has cursed the marriage relationship with a poisonous desire for control by the woman and a self-absorbed focus outside the relationship by the man.[8]

While I use the illustration of books for men and books for women, Phillips points to their respective magazines. Women's magazines are all about pleasing and staying attached to a man. Sexual performance, dieting, cooking, and so on are just the tools in the tool chest. Keeping the man is the task at hand.[9] And what about the magazines for men? They are all about the "stuff" outside relationships. When women come into it, they do so as one more object—like the rifle, or the speedboat, or the money.[10]

In short, ungoverned by grace, women want to get in closer to get the hooks into *him,* and men want to get farther away in order to get his hands onto *that.* It is not surprising—given the fact that God has determined to rule the world in this way—that feminists are continuously frustrated.

Fathers Give Bread

In the first book of the Bible, God told women that their desire would be for their husbands. This was not talking about a desire for a romantic getaway, or more time gazing into each other's eyes. It is the basis for what has been called the "war between the sexes," the battle for mastery. We have tried the unhappy expedient of letting this conflict be resolved through having one sex or the other run the show. The results have been uniformly bad. If we want out of this stand-off, we have to do it God's way. The men don't get their way, and the women don't get theirs. God should get His way.

This means that women need to recognize that feminism is one of the worst enemies that women have ever had . . . right after men. So we have to think through this issue carefully. We are not going to be able to sort out the horizontal problems we have between the sexes until we sort out the problems that both sexes have with their God in Heaven. As Calvin famously pointed out at the beginning of the *Institutes,* we cannot know God without knowing ourselves, and we cannot know ourselves without knowing God.[11]

And this is actually why feminists do not understand themselves at all. Calvin's point is a profound one, and means more than that we need to understand the triune God in order to understand the triune God. He is saying that we need to understand the triune God in order to understand ourselves, and we need to understand ourselves in order to understand the triune God. This also means that we have to understand God in order to understand our neighbor . . . in order to understand ourselves. But what if our neighbor is a member of that alien sex across the way?

The fountainhead of the Godhead is the *Father.* Women who have been hurt, neglected, and abused by men, particularly by their fathers, are women who have their understanding of their own nature shouted down by men who have taken it upon themselves to slander fatherhood. The way out is to reject the slander. Chesterton once put it this way: "Feminists are, as their name implies, opposed to anything feminine."[12] No one delights in fatherhood more than a woman at peace with her own femininity. And no one chafes at it more than a feminist does. A woman cannot be at peace with God without being at peace with the man who, together with her, bears the image of that God.

One of the great problems we have in conservative Christian circles is that of accepting slanders about the gracious character of God the Father. Liberals slander His character and reject Him for it. Conservatives actually *accept* many of the slanders, but refuse to reject Him because they know they're "not supposed to." And so they wind up worshipping—in the name of worshipping God the Father—some grotesque caricature.

When such a caricature gets into general circulation, the men and women process it differently. One of the things that women do—without strong fathers—is get weird about food. Stick with me now.

What are fathers called to? Fathers give. Fathers protect. Fathers *bestow.* Fathers yearn and long for the good of their children. Fathers delight. Fathers sacrifice. Fathers are jovial and openhanded. Fathers create abundance, and if lean times come they take the leanest portion themselves and create a sense of gratitude and abundance for the rest. Fathers love birthdays and Christmas because it provides them with yet another excuse to give some more to the kids. When fathers say no, as good fathers do from time to time, it is only because they are giving a more subtle gift, one that is a bit more complicated than a cookie. They must also include among their gifts things like self-control and discipline and a work ethic, but they are *giving* these things, not taking something else away just for the sake of taking. Fathers are not looking for excuses to say no. Their default mode is not *no*.

The canard that is frequently applied to the Puritans does not apply to the historical Puritans, but it does apply to a certain kind of dour, pinched personality. There is the kind of person who says that God is up in Heaven, looking down on us, trying to find someone who is having a good time. When He finds such a one, He tells him to stop it right *now*. H. L. Mencken defined puritanism as the haunting fear that somehow, somewhere, someone might be happy. That is, as I said, a slander on the Puritans, *but there is a kind of person that it does in fact apply to*. That kind of person fills up the lives of others with "this is bad for you," "so is that," and "so is this," and "that, too, over there." I ache for children growing up in such homes, not because they are "eating healthy" (because they usually aren't, which is another subject), but because the *spiritual* environment is so unhealthy.

What statement is being made in all this about fatherhood and provision? The kids grow up in "a garden," but not the Father's kind where all the trees are permitted but one. They grow up in something *called* a garden, where all the trees but one are forbidden, and the one that is allowed to them grows rice cake–like globules that taste like little bits of Styrofoam glued together in a nutrient ball.

And so the children are surrounded by delightful fruit that their father *could* afford, but refuses to provide them, and that other kids get to eat freely. They have a father who does not provide, although he could, which means that he must not *want* to. They have a father who does not provide, who does not bestow, who does not overflow. They come to think that God the Father is like that, and they conclude that they must not be worth very much. That sense of guilt for just existing carries over into adulthood, and they then do the same thing to their kids. We do need more guilt over actual sin, and a lot less guilt over breathing, maintaining a temperature of 98.6, and needing a certain amount of glucose for the brain. Slandering the character of God is one of the sins we need to reject *as sin.* There are people who need to start feeling guilty for feeling guilty all the time, if you follow me here.

Such folks still need to have a father who delights in them objectively. They need a father who delights in them the way Joseph delighted in Benjamin, by heaping up his plate. But with a lot of these people, that's not going to happen anytime soon. How many children in Christian homes think that the universe is governed by a pinched, censorious face *because that is the face that was presented to them?* Many Christian parents need to confront the fact that they are no fun at all, and that when the kids show up at dinner for their gruel, such a dinner is a fitting metaphor for what is going on everywhere else in that home.

The prodigal son famously veered off into excess. The older brother was a dutiful fusser. The yearning *father* was the one who had kept the fatted calf for just such an occasion as this return and directed that it be prepared for his wayward son, now repentant. Did the returning prodigal really need to go to another party? Yes, apparently he did, but it needed to happen in his *father's* house.

Many of our contemporary food oddities are little more than thinly disguised manifestations of father hunger. Of course, father hunger manifests itself in other pathological ways than food issues—sexual promiscuity, to name just one—but it is no coincidence that this era of ours, bereft of real fathers, has seen a drastic explosion of food weirdness.

Consider bread. *Fathers give bread.* "If a son shall *ask bread* of any of you *that is a father,* will he give him a stone? or if he ask a fish, will he for a fish give him a serpent?" (Luke 11:11 KJV). That is just one of the things a father is called to do. If your son asks for bread, what is your responsibility as a father? Even sinful men know that giving a stone would be a ridiculous response. But what happens these days when sons ask for bread? They don't get stones, but they frequently get some form of un-bread. And this is just a biblical and typological way of filling out a complete picture—bread from fathers, and un-bread from men acting like nonfathers.

Just as grape juice in the Lord's Supper is an anemic but fitting picture of the grape-juice gospel American evangelicals tend to preach, so also the frantic search for bread substitutes says about as loudly as anything that we are really in the market for father substitutes—which are much harder to come by, as it turns out. But we should drop the search for father substitutes, turn in repentance back to our fathers, and ask for the privilege of receiving his bread. "But when he came to himself, he said, 'How many of *my father's* hired servants *have more than enough bread,* but I perish here with hunger! I will arise *and go to my father*" (Luke 15:17–18).

This ache, this problem, this jagged hole in this generation's soul, gets into everything. There are many fruitless theological, doctrinal, and political debates that should simply be set aside for a moment so that one of the agitated participants could be asked when it was his father last hugged him.

Moses, the father of the Jewish nation, was used by God to give the children of Israel bread from heaven. And this bread from heaven was a type and an emblem of the ultimate bread from heaven, our Lord Jesus.

> Our fathers ate the manna in the wilderness; as it is written, "He gave them bread from heaven to eat." Jesus then said to them, "Truly, truly, I say to you, it was not Moses who gave you the bread from heaven, but my Father gives you the true bread from heaven." (John 6:31–32)

What does God the Father do? He gives us *true bread*. Rejection of bread, loathing of bread, the frenetic search for something that chews like it is bread but we can't let it actually *be* bread, is all, ultimately, a rejection of the Father's gift of *the* Bread. "This is the bread that came down from heaven, not like the bread the fathers ate and died. Whoever feeds on this bread will live forever" (John 6:58).

When we lose the Father, we gain wierdness, and in many areas. We discussed in an earlier chapter how a woman's identity is "much closer to home" than a man's identity is. This means that men get lost on such subjects more easily than women do. Perversions and fetishes of other kinds come much easier to men than they do women. A man's problems are much more likely to be "out there," and a woman's "in here." This is why Paul can say about a culture far advanced in decadence, that even their women were affected by it (Rom. 1:26). It takes more to pry a woman loose from her grounded sexual identity than it does a man. While there are a number of reasons why women adopt "lesbian until graduation" personas, at least one of the things we see in that phenomenon is that the heterosexual grounding is harder for women to get away from.

This also explains why self-described feminists can still get irritated with men who are not manly. The ideology that modern secularists have promulgated is an ideology that gets more "buy-in" from the men. They can bond to all kinds of things, and they do. They can project sexual desirability onto more objects outside themselves, and they do. The women have stayed closer to shore, if you will, and they still have a firmer, instinctive grasp of the ways things ought to be. So when feminists on the surface demand that men behave in a particular way, and the men say okay, this upsets the women under the surface. "Put out to sea," they say, which the men do with a will. But at the same time, the women yearn earnestly for a man who will insist on turning back to shore in order that he might take up black-dirt farming.

Questions to Consider:

1. What does Chesterton say about feminists?
2. What kind of food do fathers give their children?
3. What is pomosexuality? What kind of universe is necessary to assume in order to support that approach to sexuality?
4. What shapes our transformations and becomings?
5. Why are feminists frustrated when they get what they demand?

Chapter 12

The Fruitful Father

The Politics of Fruitfulness

"All politics is on one level sexual politics," says George Gilder.[1] To consider the sexual father as a fruitful father, we must consider, in turn, the politics of fruitfulness, and the alternative platform of calculated barrenness. We can see our culture's clear bias in three ways—the propaganda of the environmentalists, the gay agenda, and the ubiquity of porn. When we speak of the "sexual father," we are not focusing on the "tips and techniques" level.

For men, sex is not just about pleasure. It also lies at the root of a man's identity. If a society has banished that identity, or somehow made it suspect, it is not surprising that a number of men turn for reassurance to the one act that is undeniably masculine. They are trying to perform their one unquestionable male role. This is true of promiscuous men, and even of rapists. How many rapists are successful, high-achieving men? The rapist is a self-confessed loser, taking what he was not going to be given.[2]

This identity test is one that cannot be secured except by the entire culture. Because a biblical and fruitful fatherhood is challenged by our culture, it is time that Christian men answered that challenge, and answered it at the cultural level. The more children a man begets, the more mouths there are to feed, and the bigger the carbon footprint gets, and the more grief he catches from people who believe he is being irresponsible. What looks like "responsible" geopolitics—concerns about overpopulation or global warming—are actually indirect attacks on men becoming fathers. We have gotten to the point where what a man's children breathe out of their noses is considered to be a pollutant.

"In a multitude of people is the glory of a king, but without people a prince is ruined" (Prov. 14:28). This short proverb is not really ambiguous. What is being said here? As with many proverbs, the sentiments of each half of the proverb are juxtaposed. The first half of the proverb says that a large population is a glory for a king. The second half points to the disaster that awaits a political state when there is a dearth of people. The word for destruction here means "destruction"—ruination. There is a wonderful comment in 1 Chronicles of a blessing that had come to the tribe of Issachar. "Of Issachar, men who had understanding of the times, to know what Israel ought to do" (12:32). This being the case, there were no doubt lots of little kids of Issachar growing up in that same understanding.

But we live in a time when genuine fruitfulness is regarded with disingenuous suspicion. If you tell a modern New York or Seattle sophisticate that you are from Idaho or Missouri and that you have five kids, he will look at you as though you need to retreat back into your cave. In addition, we need to be reminded from time to time that the Bible is not a "spiritual" book. By this, I don't mean that the Holy Spirit didn't inspire it; rather, I mean that the dualism that we learned from modernity, the dualism that separates realms of faith and realms of reason into separate compartments, is an unholy dualism. The Bible is authoritative over all of life, and this includes the part of life that requires you to get a van instead of a small two-door. We should want to be like the men of Issachar. We are not looking at our Bibles clearly if we are not looking at our times clearly. This means that faithful biblical thinking is not *just* exegesis. When Al Gore says the world is falling apart, and that you and your five kids are a big part of the problem, you should be prepared with an answer. A man should not just beget his children; he should defend what he has done.

This is not about birth control, which I consider to be a private family matter (provided we are not talking about abortifacients). When the Scripture is silent, we want to be silent as well. Nothing here should be taken as a legalistic intrusion into the decision making of a biblical family. But at the same time, this principle also means that when Scripture speaks, we want to speak just as loudly. And the Bible says, in numerous places, that fruitfulness is a blessing (e.g., Gen. 9:1, 7; Lev. 26:9; Deut. 28:2–6; Ps. 127; 128). Like all blessings, it can be mismanaged—large families are not *automatically* happy families. A son who sleeps through harvest is a shame to his parents (Prov. 10:5), and so three sons snoring through harvest would be three times as bad. But everything else being equal, a blessing remains a blessing. The point that our passage is making, however, is that such a blessing is not just a private, family blessing. Fruitfulness is a political act.

Demographically, a given population's replacement rate is 2.1 children per couple. If that is the average, then 1,000 people today will be 1,000 people fifty years from now, and two hundred years from now. A rate significantly below that indicates that the culture is in a death spiral. Above that, the population is growing. The United States leads the developed world with a rate that is right about 2.1. Canada is at 1.5. Germany and Austria are at 1.3. Russia and Spain bring up the rear at 1.2 children per woman. So it is not enough to be doing what comes naturally; we should seek to understand it in the light of God's Word.

We have been repeatedly catechized by our secularist leaders and have been told that we have a population crisis all right—an overpopulation crisis. But what is overpopulation exactly? When a given population cannot feed itself, it would be fair to say that there are too many people. But this actually means that there are too many people who are not living under the blessing of God. The sin of unbelief looks at people as consumers. But faith sees people more as producers. After all, you were born into the world with just *one* mouth and *two* hands. What do you have when you have a population that produces more than it consumes? Wealth. What do you have when a population consumes more than it produces? Poverty—and overpopulation. But such overpopulation is caused by a *shortage* of effective workers.

When this judgment happens, when this disaster befalls a particular culture, the Lord's hand is in it. The prophet Amos asks, "Does disaster come to a city, unless the Lord has done it?" (Amos 3:6). This particular kind of ruination is not an exception. And in the modern world, we have added a twist that will make the disaster, when it finally comes, more complete and devastating. The secular West has built up a huge entitlements state, as an unquestioned ideal, which requires a young population paying into it.

Faith sees opportunity in the world that God made, and in the way God governs that world. Unbelief always sees insurmountable obstacles. Joshua and Caleb saw cities that could be conquered. The other ten spies saw cities that would be fiercely defended. And so it was to them, according to their faith. This is what Lady Wisdom says in the book of Proverbs: "By me kings reign, and rulers decree what is just. . . . All who hate me love death" (8:15, 36). And this is precisely what we see around us. The culture that rejects biblical wisdom is the culture of death and fruitlessness. Think about this for a moment. Abortion and homosexual marriage are not just cultural sins for which there *will* be judgment at the Last Day. They are sins that bring their own judgment of fruitlessness with them. When we reject the fruitfulness of life in as many ways as we have done, this is clearly an aspect of the judgment *itself*. The opposite is also true. Those who love the God of wisdom, who love Lady Wisdom, know what it is to love *life*. And this means that we must love and honor what it means to be a father.

The Wrath of Sin

When the wrath of God is revealed in the world, it is revealed as God "lets go" of a culture, allowing it to run headlong into various suicidal and fruitless practices. In this text, we find a deepening expansion of the point Paul has already made:

> For this reason God gave them up to dishonorable passions. For their women exchanged natural relations for those that are contrary to nature; and the men likewise gave up natural relations with women and were consumed with passion for one another, men committing shameless acts with men and receiving in themselves the due penalty for their error.
>
> And since they did not see fit to acknowledge God, God gave them up to a debased mind to do what ought not to be done. They were filled with all manner of unrighteousness, evil, covetousness, malice. They are full of envy, murder, strife, deceit, maliciousness. They are gossips, slanderers, haters of God, insolent, haughty, boastful, inventors of evil, disobedient to parents, foolish, faithless, heartless, ruthless. Though they know God's decree that those who practice such things deserve to die, they not only do them but give approval to those who practice them. (Rom. 1:26–32)

The wrath of God, considered here, is certainly not limited to homosexual practices. But Paul certainly places that particular perversion at the center of his argument. Notice that men do not embrace vile affections, despite everything that God could do. No, it says that God "gave them up to" these vile affections (v. 26). The reason we have gay pride parades is that *God* is doing something to us. As a result, Paul argues, even the women gave up the natural use of man (v. 26). And the men did the same, turning in unseemly desire toward one another (v. 27). Just as they did not want to retain God in their knowledge, so God let them not retain Him in their knowledge (v. 28). As a result, they then filled up with all kinds of spiritual sludge (vv. 29–31). Sins are like grapes; they come in bunches. This happened despite the fact that they knew it to be the judgment of God (v. 32). This means their suppression of the knowledge of God did not really work. They did not want to retain the knowledge of God, but they still knew the judgment of God (v. 32). That judgment is that sin warrants death, as they well know, but they insist on becoming cheerleaders for that way of death (v. 32).

We have seen a number of times that God created mankind, male and female, in His own image (Gen. 1:27). This means that attempts to rearrange how everything goes are foundational attempts at trying to make a heretical theology stick. By defacing the image, we assault the reality. By rearranging the components, rebellious mankind is trying to re-create God, trying to make Him into something other than what He is. Homosexual actions are therefore a high-profile revolt against the Trinity. All sins do the same, but this reveals the problem in stark relief. We are at war with the image we see, but the only thing we can strike is the mirror.

Recall also that God does not just reveal Himself in Scripture. He reveals Himself in nature, and the natural use of the female for the male, and the natural use of the male for the female, is an important part of that revelation. Homosexual practice is contrary to the design of God, not just because God says so in Scripture (Lev. 20:13), which He of course does, but also because we discover in the natural world that *the parts don't fit*. This is not just physiological, although it is that. If you keep all the nuts in one bag and all the bolts in another, you won't ever build anything. But "the parts" don't fit anywhere else either. They don't fit spiritually, mentally, emotionally, or culturally. Homosexual advocates like to represent this point as a cheap laugh line from "traditionalists," but Paul shows it to be a cogent point, an unanswerable argument.

When Paul says that God gave them up to a debased mind, he does not just mean that they are vile from our perspective, though others might differ. Remember that this is at the very center of God's judgment. When men desired to think as though God were not there, God granted their wish *in judgment* and gave them over to a reprobate mind. This is how we know that wrath is occurring—God gives them up, God gives them over (Rom. 1:26, 28). Paul is echoing the judgment themes found in Psalm 106, where we see that God granted the Israelites their request, but He sent leanness to their souls (v. 15). God judges in wrath by saying yes.

The sins that follow are not just sins that the culture in question dabbles in. They don't just happen from time to time. When God's wrath is being poured out, what happens? The *pouring* corresponds to a *filling*. "Being filled with all unrighteousness . . ." This particular cultural jug is filled with all unrighteousness, sexual uncleanness, wickedness of various kinds, covetousness and *wanting*, malice and spite, green envy, murder of course, disputes and tangles, lies and more lies, a surly malignity, whispering campaigns, backstabbing, God-hating, contempt for others, overweening arrogance, boasting and bragging, evil inventions, disobedience to parents, stupidity and stupor, oath-breaking, without natural affection, hard-hearted, and unmerciful. And please note the ironic twist, in the modern parlance, to oppose the root that produces all this corrupt fruit is now called "hate." Yeah, right, whatever.

Those who know God suppress the knowledge of God in unrighteousness, but nevertheless retain their awareness of the judgment of God (under which they live), and yet persist in their rebellion. They know that sin is worthy of death, but nevertheless do them, and *take pleasure* when others follow the way of death along with it. And this is how we know that America is under judgment. Note again, we do not know in the abstract that America, like all nations, is headed for judgment *if*... We are dealing with a very concrete situation, not an abstract one. Suppose there was a nation awash in consumer goods, a nation that gained the world but lost its own soul (Matt. 16:26). Suppose that nation cut off its future by slaughtering more than forty million of her own citizens. Suppose further that this was urged as a noble and constitutional thing to do. Suppose that nation began to sanctify sodomite marriages and laughed at every form of righteousness. And suppose there were millions of Christians in this country who falsely longed for the nation to deliver herself by returning to her noble, true self, instead of longing for Christ to save her from her corrupted, wicked self.

So fathers are urged to be fruitless by "going green." And fathers are urged to be fruitless by seeking out sexual partners who are as infertile as a mule. And to deal with the remainder, there is always porn. One of the things that should be most obvious to a man about the women involved in pornography is that such images, however appealing a man might find them, are images that can present him with no children. They are barren. They flaunt their breasts, but they will never nurse the children of those who gawk at them. The men who pursue such women are men who want such barrenness; they find it a selling point. Another way of saying this is that they don't want to be fathers. They want the privileges of sexual release (after a fashion) but without the responsibilities that God's wisdom necessarily attached to these pleasures.

Scripture frequently speaks of wickedness in terms of its fruitlessness—false teachers are "fruitless trees in late autumn, twice dead, uprooted" (Jude 12). Not only do the wicked embrace the ethic of fruitlessness, they are also openly hostile to those who are fruitful. This is what helps explain the comments that women with a band of small children have to encounter at the mall. "Do you know what causes that?" My daughter, mother of six, has been tempted to reply, "Yes, and it looks like I am getting a whole lot more of it than you are."

The purpose of farming is not to work on your tan, or to keep your weight down—even though farming does help with both. The point of farming is food, and the biological purpose of sexual relations is children. And speaking of food, we may be grateful that God invested food with the glories of taste and flavor, but the point of food remains nourishment for the body.

Another way of coming to this point is by saying that sexual relations need to be tied in a general way to the possibilities of fatherhood in order to maintain the glory that God designed. This excludes calculated fruitlessness, as we have been discussing, but it also excludes planting crops in soon-to-be abandoned fields.

I recall a conversation I had at a bus stop one morning when I was in junior high. Another boy was there, boasting in his father's sexual exploits across the Pacific during the Second World War. No telling, the boy informed us, how many brothers and sisters he had scattered across that part of the world. His story made me sick, but not because his father had broken an abstract goody-goody rule that I had learned about in Sunday school. The story made me sick *because I had a father that I thought the world of, and who knew my name*. One of the best things a father can do to prevent his sons from drifting into immorality is to connect sex and fatherhood. The thought of all those kids growing up without a dad was really distressing to me. About the only thing that would have made it worse would be for me to be that nameless dad to one of those ditched children.

Questions to Consider:

1. Are children an automatic blessing?
2. Why should true fathers love fruitfulness?
3. What is a good definition of overpopulation?
4. What two sins are a good example of judgments in themselves?
5. What can fathers do to protect their sons from future immorality?

Chapter 13

Some Father Mechanics

Obedience Therefore

The most important word in the book of Ephesians is *therefore*. It lies right at the hinge between the first three chapters and the last three chapters. "I *therefore*, a prisoner for the Lord, urge you to walk in a manner worthy of the calling to which you have been called" (Eph. 4:1). The first three chapters were filled with grand indicatives, with nothing to do but believe them or not. The last three chapters are filled with imperatives, requirements, and commands. If the last three chapters are detached from the first three, this has the effect of detaching ethics from gospel, and what a death trap that is.

In a similar way, this chapter contains a number of practical pointers for fathers. But if they are detached from some of the broader issues contained within this book, the effect will be a paint-by-numbers approach to fathering, which never really works very well. So, "practical" is all very well and good, but it should never be separated from the larger context. The point is not to get young people to grit their teeth and conform to the standard. The task before us is to bring up our children in such a way as to love the standard. This is not possible to do with externally driven rules. It is a function of loyalty, and loyalty is based on love and relationship. We should consider what this looks like from the child's perspective first.

> *Hear, my son, your father's instruction,*
> *and forsake not your mother's teaching,*
> *for they are a graceful garland for your head*
> *and pendants for your neck.* (Prov. 1:8–9)

> *My son, do not forget my teaching,*
> *but let your heart keep my commandments,*
> *for length of days and years of life*
> *and peace they will add to you.*
> *Let not steadfast love and faithfulness forsake you;*
> *bind them around your neck;*
> *write them on the tablet of your heart.*
> *So you will find favor and good success*
> *in the sight of God and man.* (Prov. 3:1–4)

> *My son, do not lose sight of these—*
> *keep sound wisdom and discretion,*
> *and they will be life for your soul*
> *and adornment for your neck.* (Prov. 3:21–22)

> *My son, keep your father's commandment,*
> *and forsake not your mother's teaching.*
> *Bind them on your heart always;*
> *tie them around your neck.*

When you walk, they will lead you;
when you lie down, they will watch over you;
and when you awake, they will talk with you. (Prov. 6:20–22)

In the texts quoted, there is a great deal of material—more than we can address here. What I would like to do is draw out one basic theme. First, the instruction of a father and the law of a mother should be treated as a garland of *grace* for the head, and as an ornamental chain *around the neck* (Prov. 1:9). Second, a young person should take care to bind steadfast love and faithfulness *around his neck,* and he does this by not forgetting his father's law, and by cultivating a heart that keeps his commandments (Prov. 3:3). The result is a blessed life, the kind everyone can see. Third, sound wisdom and discretion is life to the soul and an adornment *around the neck* (Prov. 3:22). And last, a man should take up the commandments of his father, and not abandon the law of his mother. Tie them onto your heart, and hang them *around your neck.* These are not good-luck charms, but Solomon almost speaks of them as though they were. But this is *blessing* from a personal Father, not luck in an impersonal universe. This is the triune God of all grace, and not some rabbit's foot.

Obedience to parents is therefore a young person's *glory.* What should a teen do with what his parents have asked? He should not trudge off reluctantly, muttering to himself, slamming doors as he goes. No, the standard set forth in Scripture is for him to take what he has been asked to do and hang it around his neck as he would an Olympic gold medal that he has just won. If an athlete comes in first in the Olympics, he does not stuff the medal into his gym bag and slouch off halfway through the national anthem. Not at all. What do you do with your glory? Glad obedience is glorious.

Some will of course worry that this emphasis will turn children into brain-dead clones. And there is a kind of authoritarianism in some fathers that has that effect. But what we are talking about is much more biblical, and it actually has been done before. Historian Steven Ozment points out the balance that was achieved in the Reformation in their approach to child-rearing.

> By their inculcation of individual religious certitude and their incessant ridicule of unscriptural, hypocritical, and merely external religious practices, Protestant catechisms, so carefully designed to teach the child to obey, were at the same time programming him to defy. Heroism as well as subservience filled their catechisms.[1]

So this is not a life of ease for parents, and the glory of raw obedience for teenagers, an obedience that drops mysteriously out of the sky. It does not work this way. Obedience, of the kind described here, arises from personal loyalty, and this loyalty arises from love. Where does love come from? As always, God models it for us. What He asks us to do, He *shows* us how to do. And we love Him because He loved us first (1 John 4:19). And if we want our young people to love us, with grace around the neck, then we must show them how it is worn. This means, not so incidentally, that fathers should begin all this with their own fathers, not with their sons.

Loving the Standard

If you cannot get the kids to love the standard, then lower the standard. I am not talking about God's commandments (His standards), which we have no authority to lower, but rather addressing the questions that surround what might be called house rules. Lower the standard to the point where everyone in the family can pitch in together. This is not actually lowering standards, but rather raising the parental standard, which is the real reason we don't like it.

Fathers must embrace the task of communicating, in a contagious way, love for the standard.

Some parents might protest that this is impossible. But what does this example teach the young people in the home? It teaches them that nobody around here has to do "impossible" things, and since the requirement to make your bed, or to comb your hair, or to stop texting so much, are all clearly impossible, then they don't have to be done. If you want your children to be obedient, *then show them how.* Giving up when it seems "impossible" is not showing them how it is done. Apart from a context of love and loyalty, fatherly discipline is just clobbering a kid. And since clobbering a kid is not what God said to do, the child is learning the *fundamental* lesson that, in this house, we don't have to do what God says to do. Instead, we learn to be sneaky enough to not get clobbered.

Each member of the family is supposed to understand that the whole family is a unit. All the members are on the same team. If a family has drifted into an adversarial set of roles, then the parents have to do something to stop the game or maybe change the rules. They have to do *something* that works. Let us suppose the whole family is flunking high school calculus. Wouldn't it be far better to all go back to sixth grade and pass that grade *together?* We have to remember that the standard set in the above passages from Proverbs is not an impossible standard. That was not written for angels in Heaven. It was written for us. These things are set before us now. There will be more on loving the standard in a subsequent chapter.

The hardest thing to maintain in this unbalanced world is balance. We react, we pull away, we lurch, and we tumble. We do this in many ways. And, having heard the exhortation that we should teach our children to love the standard, but if they don't then we should lower the standard, what temptation will confront us? The temptation will be to think that laziness and apathy are grace, and that defensiveness when confronted is zeal for the law of God. But loving God with all your mind, soul, heart, and strength is a love with *balance*.

> Children, obey your parents in the Lord, for this is right. "Honor your father and mother" (this is the first commandment with a promise), "that it may go well with you and that you may live long in the land." Fathers, do not provoke your children to anger, but bring them up in the discipline and instruction of the Lord. (Eph. 6:1–4)

Here are some of the basics of Christian living within the family. We begin with the duty of obedience. When children are young and living at home, honor entails obedience, necessarily. When children are grown and out on their own, the duty of honor remains, but it is rendered differently (Mark 7:10–13). This is obedience rendered by children in the Lord. The word for *obedience* could be rendered literally as "listen under"—or, as we might put it, "listen up." This attentiveness to what parents say is described here by Paul as a form of honor, and he goes on to describe how much of a blessing it will be to the children who are taught by their parents how to behave in this way. This commandment, to honor parents, is the first commandment with a promise. The promise from God Himself is that things will go well for you throughout your long life on the earth (Eph. 6:3). And then fathers are presented with an alternative—one thing is prohibited and another is enjoined. Fathers are told not to exasperate their children to the point of wrath or anger, and instead are told to bring them up in the nurture and admonition of the Lord. Note that they are not told to provoke their children to anger *with* the nurture and admonition of the Lord—one excludes the other.

One of the things fathers can stop doing (that provokes children) is to stop experimenting on them. In construction work, one of the good things about a concrete pour is that, no matter what, a couple hours later, you're all done. This is also one of the really bad things about it. You don't want to start out with a long foundation wall and wind up with a patio. Kids are a concrete pour. The time they will spend in your home goes by a lot faster than you initially thought it would. Fathers are tasked with the responsibility of bringing them up in the Lord, which means that fathers are tasked with the responsibility of *working in harmony with the nature of the child*. It is, of course, debated what that nature is actually like, and so how are parents to deal with this?

Too many Christian parents are like that old joke about the Harvard man. "You can always tell a Harvard man, but you can't tell him much." Because we have successfully established the principle that parents have true authority in the home, many foolish parents have concluded that this means that *anything* they may happen to think about child rearing, or education, or nutrition, or training, or courtship standards, is therefore *automatically* blessed of God. But fathers are told not to provoke their children, because in this fallen world, *this is a very easy thing to do*. This is a very easy thing for *Christian* fathers to do. If it had not been an easy temptation for Ephesian fathers, Paul could have saved his advice for the occasional dad who really needed it. Paul does not make the mistake of thinking that authority makes folly impossible—he cautions against authoritative folly.

The hallmark of whether or not a father is experimenting on his kids, as opposed to bringing them up in obedience, is how open he is to the idea of someone else actually measuring what he is doing. How open is he to true accountability? "Not that we dare to classify or compare ourselves with some of those who are commending themselves. But when they measure themselves by one another and compare themselves with one another, they are without understanding" (2 Cor. 10:12). Note that phrase "without understanding." How can you tell if parents have undertaken their solemn responsibilities as parents with a demeanor of humble confidence? "Let a righteous man strike me—it is a kindness; let him rebuke me—it is oil for my head; let my head not refuse it" (Ps. 141:5). The question can be easily answered. How open is he to outside accountability? If he wants his children to have high levels of accountability, while he himself has virtually none, then this is the way to a bad family disaster.

The Christian faith is a road, sure enough. But it is also a *way*. This means that *how* we walk is as important as *where* we walk. If someone has questions about what a man is doing, it does not answer the concern to point at the road. It does not answer to bring out various books and websites that argue for this particular kind of asphalt. That's as may be, but there is something else going on. How does a father conjugate the verb *firm*? Does he say, *I am firm, you are stubborn, he is pig-headed*? If he does this easily, then he has wandered from the way, whatever road he is on.

Discipline As Gift and Gratitude

Another way of measuring this is by whether or not a man requires obedience of his children for *their* sake or not. If he doesn't require it at all, that is selfish. If he demands it for his own reasons, that is selfish also. If he requires it as a gift to them and for them, then he is modeling the same kind of obedience he is asking for.

Of course, there is no way for any thoughtful father to hear these words without conviction. And conviction is good. But always remember there is a hard-riding guilt that is from the enemy of our souls, and not from the Holy Spirit. Remember that as God is teaching us not to provoke others with impossible standards, He models this for us. *He* is not provoking us with impossible standards either.

Our Father in Heaven requires nothing in this that He does not do Himself. He is the Father of all grace. The one thing to remember about this grace is that He—precisely because He is a loving Father—requires us to freely extend what we have freely received (Matt. 10:8; Col. 3:13).

So let us consider how this general demeanor applies to a very practical sample problem. One of the most vexing questions for fathers bringing up kids in this tawdry world is the matter of entertainment standards and how to protect his family from the rising levels of crassness we see everywhere. But one of the running temptations we encounter in this world is the temptation of coming up with makeshift forms of holiness. We *think* we know what God wants, and we bustle around to come up with some form of that on our own. But then we discover later, to our dismay, that this is not what He was asking for at all.

Compare these two passages from Ephesians:

> Let the thief no longer steal, *but rather* let him labor, doing honest work with his own hands, so that he may have something to share with anyone in need. (4:28)

> But sexual immorality and all impurity or covetousness must not even be named among you, as is proper among saints. Let there be no filthiness nor foolish talk nor crude joking, which are out of place, *but instead* let there be thanksgiving. (5:3–4)

There is an important word that is found in both of these texts. That is the word rendered as *rather* or *instead* (*mallon*), a word Paul uses in exactly the same way in both texts. In the first instance, his use of it is not really that surprising to us. In the second, there are perhaps quite a few surprises in store. In the first example, Paul says that a thief should stop stealing and that instead of this he should get an honest job, working with his hands. This is because in Paul's mind there is a basic alternative here—stealing or working. If you work and generate a surplus for sharing with those in need, then you have filled up your life with that which will exclude the practice of stealing. We should note in passing that Paul does not tell the thief to get a job so that he can make his own money, and then be in a position to tell hippies to "get a job." Honest work enables providing for one's own needs, and for *sharing*.

But Paul argues in exactly the same way a few verses later when he teaches the Ephesians how to get free of crass joking, covetous grasping, the easy naming of fornication and uncleanness, and so forth. The impure life is to be replaced with . . . now here is where we would say "the pure life as described by Mrs. Grundy," but Paul says "with thanksgiving." We contrast impurity with purity, but Paul contrasts impurity with contentment. There is something deep going on here. This is not a trivial point.

Biblical contentment is not stoicism. We are not called to be content in the same way that a block of wood is content—even though we may assume that the wood presumably *is* content. That is not what we are called to. And Paul is not urging us into some kind of "happy, happy, happy all the day" kind of stuff. He is not urging a constant and frothy giddiness. No, he sets the pattern for us, providing us with an example. In one place he describes himself as "sorrowful, yet always rejoicing" (2 Cor. 6:10). His joy, his contentment, was not a perverse kind of denial, or a stiff-upper-lip stoicism. And yet it *was* "always rejoicing." This kind of contentment, whether well fed or hungry, is a deep satisfaction with the will of God for you (Phil. 4:11–12). This is bedrock stuff—a basalt kind of joy twenty feet down. And it needs to be a foundational, bedrock joy that runs underneath the entire house.

A few verses later Paul tells us that we must, always and for everything, give thanks in the name of Jesus—"giving thanks always *and for everything*" (Eph. 5:20). This is part of his sustained argument, where he is continuing to show us the contrast, not between dirty and clean, but between dirty and *grateful*. This is what helps us to name the problem rightly.

For example, if you are fighting a losing battle for godly entertainment standards at your house, the problem is not teen sex comedies; the problem is discontent. The problem is not dirty jokes, but frustration. If an authority figure says, "You should tell clean jokes instead of dirty jokes," this is a perfect setup for the comeback, "But clean jokes are *lame*." But Paul doesn't tell us to fight dirty jokes with clean jokes, lame or not. He says to fight dirty jokes with contentment and gratitude. And for those who see the world biblically, they see that those whose talk is full of corruption are *not* revealing a worldly wise sophistication, but rather a seething and unhappy discontent.

Just as the thief is trying to get something the easy way instead of God's way, so also the person with a foul mouth is trying to get satisfaction in his own way. But outside of Jesus Christ, there can be no deep satisfaction—and in Christ, everything is pure. So if we are trying to find satisfaction independently of Him, that move will always veer toward the crass, the filthy, the immoral, the disturbing, and the rest of that fetid swamp. But it makes no sense for someone to live in the swamp of discontent with a resolve to "keep it clean." Keeping it clean is arbitrary, given the quagmire of discontent he lives on, and on top of that, keeping it clean there is impossible.

"Keeping a rule," however technically correct, falls easily into the trap of abstraction and impersonalism. For a father to "make rules" for a discontent household is simply sweeping water uphill. Adjusting the environment is radically insufficient. Too many fathers deny the need for the gospel in how they try to protect their children from sin. You cannot adjust the environment in such a way to keep sin out. This would include school, church, books, television, diet, and so on. Christian faithfulness does not come from rearranging the furniture.[2]

As a result, we oppose sin with a false standard of holiness, and then are surprised at its impotence. But gratitude, thanksgiving, contentment, and joy are always personal, by definition. Jesus is there, and if you thank Him, then that gratitude fills up all the available space. This is the "gratitude displacement" strategy. Scripture teaches us that gratitude and thanksgiving are central to a right relationship with God, which in turn is central to a right relationship to the world around us. The fundamental problem with the unregenerate heart and mind is that it will not honor God as God, and will not give Him thanks (Rom. 1:21). Contrary to this, we want to make sure we do both. Confronting sin, we should approach it with gratitude displacement.

When a child is disciplined, one of the ways you can tell if the home environment is what it ought to be is by whether or not the first instinct of the child is to turn back to his father for a restoration of fellowship. If he does, then this means the general climate is one of fellowship, which the sin and discipline disrupted, and which the child wants to have restored. But if the response to the discipline is anger, sullenness, and so forth, this is an indication that the discipline was acute pain that interrupted a larger pattern of chronic pain. The child does not try to restore fellowship because he does not have a good idea of what that might be.

That said, a refusal to discipline is a way of insulting God. "Why then do you scorn my sacrifices and my offerings that I commanded, and honor your sons above me by fattening yourselves on the choicest parts of every offering of my people Israel?" (1 Sam. 2:29).

If a child is spoiled as a child, when he is grown, he *stays* spoiled.

"His father had never at any time displeased him by asking, 'Why have you done thus and so?' He was also a very handsome man, and he was born next after Absalom" (1 Kings 1:6).

And here is a cluster of proverbs that tell us, in no uncertain terms, that discipline is a good thing. Fathers, in order to be true fathers, must discipline. "Discipline your son, and he will give you rest; he will give delight to your heart" (Prov. 29:17). "Do not withhold discipline from a child; if you strike him with a rod, he will not die. If you strike him with the rod, you will save his soul from Sheol" (Prov. 23:13–14). "The rod and reproof give wisdom, but a child left to himself brings shame to his mother" (Prov. 29:15).

But we should also be able to tell at a glance that harsh and domineering fathers can find these texts—and others like them—and focus on them in such a way as to turn the whole world gray.[3] It is as though they found the prohibited tree in the garden of Eden, built a fence around that alone, and acted as if it were the whole garden. True discipline says *no* in a world full of *yes*. And this is done in such a way that a child growing up in this context of life-giving discipline understands the whole process, as well as understanding what he has been delivered from.[4] "The teaching of the wise is a fountain of life, that one may turn away from the snares of death" (Prov. 13:14).

Balance Is Foundational

> Conservative Protestant theological assumptions about the nature of God the Father and of Jesus Christ thus give shape to a model of human fatherhood that encompasses, on the one hand, love, abiding concern, and mercy, and on the other, authority, justice, and sufficient severity to engender fear in a child.[5]

So as a father undertakes the responsibility of really fathering his children, even those who are already showing signs of defiance, he should guard against four basic temptations—a feeling of impotence and helplessness, a mistaken belief that indulgence is grace, the prideful desire to save face, and a mistaken belief that an adversarial harshness and severity is law.

Fathers who are first coming to grips with their responsibilities in a child's defiance and rebellion will have to sort through well-meaning attempts at comfort that many Christian friends will offer. They will also have to learn how to reject the same suggestions that proceed from every person's natural inclination to self-justification. That false comfort runs like this: we are of course sad about our son's condition, and it grieves us, but it is a misfortune for all of us, and not something that any one person, father or mother, can be held responsible for.

But while there is certainly grief that is experienced over such a situation, it is a different kind of grief than what a person would be going through if he discovered he had, say, inoperable cancer. This grief is the grief of shame, and shame in the Bible is not separated from connectedness and responsibility. This point really is a simple one to establish, but it is a hard point to make stick because shame is a state of mind and heart that we dislike so intensely that we will go through all kinds of emotional convolutions to get out of it.

However, the Scriptures say that laziness in a son is a shame to his parents (Prov. 10:5). A son can be outdone by a faithful servant, causing shame (Prov. 17:2). A son who rejects his parents causes shame and brings reproach (Prov. 19:26). And all of it proceeds from a parental refusal to teach the child wisdom early on (Prov. 29:15).

So the bottom line is that when a father is first coming to grips with his responsibility for how his son or daughter is currently behaving, he should not allow the well-intentioned words of his kind-hearted Christian friends to trump what Scripture says.

But at the same time, these (admittedly hard) words from Scripture were not given in order to rub our noses in it, they are given because true repentance is the beginning of all restoration. That is the goal here. But true repentance for fathers cannot happen without them *owning* it. If we want our children to take responsibility, *we should begin by showing them how it is done.*

The second simple point to make is that when the Bible talks about the qualifications for ministry, among other qualifications, it tells us that households are ruled, *managed* (1 Tim. 3:4–5). They can be managed poorly or well. When they are ruled well, the children are submissive to their father. When they are not ruled well, we may fully expect the mismanagement to carry over into the church if such a man were to be ordained. If a man's son is not in subjection to his father, with all seriousness, but simply laughs when his father tries to rein him in, what conclusion can be drawn from this?

In a world where excuses were not so quickly offered, it would not be necessary to go over this, and I am sorry that I have to. But for a struggling family, hard truth is far better than soft comfort. One of the best things a father in a challenging situation can do is reject, as a temptation, a feeling of impotence or irrelevance.

But another problem is out there as well, which is the view that virtually anything can be fixed with a hug. America has been largely Oprahfied, and it is a message that sells well. "Just love on 'em," and that should fix it. Over the years my wife and I have referred to the problem of a child having a "low tank," meaning that it was time for us to pour on the affection. But this, like everything else in this sorry world, can be misconstrued and misapplied.

When a kid has a low tank, he is low on what he needs from mom and dad. She is low on what the parents ought to be giving. But to simply assume that the only possible thing needed is "daddy dates" is a recipe for spoiling a kid. We have already noted that the context of faithful child rearing is warmth and affection. Grace contains law, just as the garden of Eden contained a prohibited tree. But it was not a garden full of prohibited trees, with one solitary available tree in the middle. Grace is the larger context, but limits are there for a reason. We already discussed the example of a checkbook. When a father writes a major check, he needs to do this in the context of having deposited way more than *that* amount in her account over the years. If he has not done this, the check won't clear.

But there are different mistakes that fathers make with regard to this. One is the mistake already mentioned made by the austere father, who thinks that he can't be out of money because he still has some checks left. But indulgent daddies make the opposite mistake. They think that if they dispense enough daddy time, if they are consistently warm and affectionate, if they are approachable and sensitive males, then it follows from this that they will never have to write a check. They have all kinds of money in the account, but they don't have the courage to spend any of it.

In my role as pastor, I have sometimes asked daughters who have gotten into some kind of significant trouble what their relationship with their dad is like. Often the answer is the obvious one of a distant and harsh man. But not infrequently the answer is that the daughter thinks her dad is a sweetie pie. "Oh, we are really close," she might say. She does not go on to add that he is a pushover, but she might as well have.

Children need fathers to be *fathers*. They need fathers to draw a line, to set a boundary. They need limits. But they also need these limits from a man who has established his wisdom in drawing them. The limits are not set for their own sake, but for the child's sake. And they are not set all by themselves, but are balanced in the context of a gracious relationship—just as the numbers on checks should be balanced in the context of the numbers on deposit slips.

Holding Pride Under

Another problem is pride. Say that a young son is acting up in public settings and it embarrasses his father. The father knows there is a serious problem, and he finds himself frequently making generic excuses to people, but he doesn't *do* anything that will actually address the problem. He is not trying to help his son, but rather trying to smooth over awkward social situations for *himself*. Say that he asks his son to do something, and the son just stares for a moment and turns away. He ignores his dad, and so then dad ignores his ignoring. After the son is gone, dad makes a lame joke to a friend about how the boy was up late last night and can be a real pain in the rear end when that happens.

The central problem in this situation is pride—the father's. There are people in his circle of friends or in his extended family who see the problem, and the causes of it, and who could very likely give him genuine, pointed help. But because of pride, these are the very people he is most likely to make excuses to, and the least likely to ask for advice. He admires them, and their abilities with their children, and so he is trying to *prove* something to them instead of *learning* from them.

If the topic ever comes up, the father may acknowledge that he has *something* of a problem, or a *measure* of difficulty, but he doesn't humble himself completely. Because of this, the people who could really help don't say everything they could; or they do and dad doesn't hear it; or they do say it and he hears it, but the next day his pride is back full force and most of their counsel is displaced by it.

A father's pride should not be the one barrier that prevents him from hearing from others what he truly needs to hear and from learning what he needs to learn. I am not talking about him listening to the people who *think* they know what the problem is—I am talking about the people whom *the father* knows understand what the problem is.

Abdication by fathers can cause extreme situations. A son is out of control, and his parents feel helpless. His father doesn't know what to do. If dad tells him to do something and he doesn't feel like it, he throws down and there you are. He is defiant, he says that he hates everybody, and we can predict the rest of the drill.

And yet Scripture says the one who refuses to discipline his son hates his son. "Whoever spares the rod hates his son, but he who loves him is diligent to discipline him" (Prov. 13:24). Yes, the reply might come that "we don't know how to spank," or "whenever I have tried it, the whole thing turns into an even bigger disaster than what we have now." In some cases, it seems that the only thing God *wants* to have happen is the making of paternal excuses.

Two things: First, those who know the situation and who see it with biblical wisdom see that the son is pleading for someone to love him enough to draw limits and enforce them. It may seem that he sure doesn't *act* like he is pleading for anything. He acts like he is demanding the world and everything in it. Sure, but the logic still makes sense. How outrageous and out of control does he have to get before someone will love him enough to intervene? The more outrageous the behavior, the easier it is for parents to think that no one can do anything. But the more outrageous the behavior is, *he* might think, the more it proves that absolutely *nothing* will get someone to love him.

And second, the plea of ignorance won't wash. If parents don't know how to handle this, then they should find out. If the son had a rare form of cancer, would flipping through the yellow pages for five minutes be sufficient to discharge all parental duties ("we looked for treatment providers but came up short")? *No*. If the parents don't know how to deal with this difficult situation, then they should find somebody who does. They should move if they need to. They shouldn't stop looking until they find someone.

But holding pride under is not as easy as it might seem. If the answer to the problem were obvious, then the oldest son wouldn't be an out-of-control discipline case, and the youngest daughter wouldn't be such a needy bucket. Now, precisely because the exact nature of the problem is *not* obvious, when the parents first seek out the input of someone who has biblical wisdom on these things, the chances are the advice will have two characteristics. First, it will probably be surprising. Often, an outsider's input will tell the father to do the exact opposite of what he thought he was supposed to be doing—like trying to explain to a Southerner how to drive in snow. He has been trying to turn the wheel this way, but he actually should be trying to turn it a different way. Many aspects of this problem are because of the counterintuitive nature of the solution.

Another aspect of this outside input is a little more unpleasant. When parents finally get real help from someone who is willing to be honest about what is going on in their family, and how they got to where they are, it is in the highest degree likely that father or mother, or both, will be offended. Part of the reason why they have gotten this far without hearing what they need to hear is that many of their friends instinctively know this. The temptation for the struggling parent will be to think that the person who finally speaks up "doesn't understand," or "has a simplistic approach," or "doesn't know the family dynamics," and so on. And the longer it takes for someone to finally say something, the more it seems like an intervention when it finally does happen.

I am not saying that such an outside observer is perfect or omniscient. My point is that when parents don't know why their son is out of control, someone else is likely to have a better grasp of understanding why than they do. And even if he doesn't, what good does it do for the parents to get offended? The temptation to take offense in a situation like this should be taken as a version of that children's game, where you tell the child he is getting warmer, warmer, warmer, until he finds the button. The more prickly and offended you feel yourself getting, the more godly advice is probably getting warmer, warmer, warmer. So fight the temptation to take offense. Roll with it.

And when a child is out of control, this is because the parents have often made the mistake of slipping into an adversarial role, instead of what they ought to be occupying, which is a watchful and parental role. The first unfortunate step in becoming an adversary to your child is that of *taking it personally.* When a two-year-old is defiant, you certainly have a problem to solve. But what you don't have is an enemy. If you slip into an adversarial role, what you are doing is *creating* an adversary within the home.

The collisions that occur when a child is small are often the means that parents unwittingly use to name their child as *trouble,* thus teaching him that this is his role, this is his name, this is his destiny. "Why can't you be more like your brother?" is offered as an exasperated question, while it is often heard by the child as a statement that if he is to retain his *own* name, he must continue to do what he is doing.

There is something counterintuitive here, something that fathers with problem children must embrace as the first step away from the problem. However much a child's behavior is displeasing to him, a father has to come to grips with the fact that the behavior is something that, at some level, his father has *required* of him. This is another way of saying that the first step out is confession, not accusation. If the child is an adversary, then bring accusations. But if your child is still your child, as he is, then the place to begin is confession. A father doesn't have to confess *how* he required this of him (because he doesn't know that yet), but he should confess to God as sin the fact that he did require this of him.

A man might wonder how it is possible to have a rebellious and out-of-control son when he has not ever thought of himself as an indulgent father. It is right to see that radical indulgence on the part of a father is a disaster for the kids—children need direction, counsel, admonition, and correction. Of course they do. And if a father does not provide this, the child grows up rudderless. That being the case, other more powerful voices will step in to provide direction. Those voices can best be categorized under the heading of lusts. But rebellion in children can come from another direction as well. If a father's disposition is negative, if he provides *nothing but* direction, counsel, admonition, and correction, then the father has become nothing but *law* to his child. And what does law do when it comes into contact with sinners? It reveals sin (Rom. 3:20). More than this, it *provokes* sin (Rom. 5:20). A good example of this is Kathleen Parker's humorous reaction to righteous fussers: "Even though I favor the mom 'n' pop model, pious pronouncements from the religious always-Right make me want to pierce my tongue and join a transsexual commune."[6]

This is why Ecclesiastes tells us not to be overly righteous. Why should you destroy yourself (7:16)? In contrast, grace *deals* with sin. Indulgence does not. Law would like to, but cannot. To cover up for its impotence, law in a father can deliver yet one more disapproving lecture. And the son concludes that if he is going to be hanged for a thief no matter what he does, he might as well steal something. Gracious fathers lead their sons through the minefield of sin. Indulgent fathers watch their sons wander off into the minefield. Legal fathers chase them there.

It is not possible for a child to get any of this if his father is not getting it. The ambience of obedience is something that is caught, not merely taught.

> I do not write these things to make you ashamed, but to admonish you as my beloved children. For though you have countless guides in Christ, you do not have many fathers. For I became your father in Christ Jesus through the gospel. I urge you, then, be imitators of me. That is why I sent you Timothy, my beloved and

> faithful child in the Lord, to remind you of my ways in Christ, as I teach them everywhere in every church. (1 Cor. 4:14–17)

So Paul begged the Corinthians to imitate him. In the verse prior he identifies himself as more than a teacher. He was their father. The way children really follow a father is by means of imitation. As dearly loved children, Paul says elsewhere, be imitators of God (Eph. 5:1). Children imitate. In this passage, we also see that imitation can work at a distance. Timothy was a dearly loved son to Paul, and he sent Timothy to be with the Corinthians so that they could see Paul's reflection in him. As a beloved son, he had imitated Paul. Paul knew this: Timothy was "faithful in the Lord." Consequently, he was in a position to remind them of Paul's way of life, and Paul's way of life was something he taught in all the churches.

The Christian life is a *way*, and it is a way that must be *copied* if we are to understand it rightly. "The beauty of a well-governed family will be seen, in this manner, to be a kind of silent, natural-looking power; as if it were a matter only of growth, and could never have been otherwise."[7] And that is it—the beauty of a well-governed family.

Questions to Consider:

1. How can the book of Ephesians be divided? Why is this important?
2. How should a father's standards be worn by his son?
3. What is the father's task with regard to the standard he requires of his children?
4. Why does Paul caution fathers against provoking their children?
5. What does it mean to say America has been Oprahfied?

Chapter 14

Our Father

The Forgotten Father

Theology undergirds everything. How we think of God the Father will drive how we think of all fathers. God the Father provides the ultimate definition of what a father should in fact be like. The good news provided in the Christian message is that Jesus is the way, the truth, and the life—no man comes to the *Father* except through Him. And this is good news indeed.

In some respects, this chapter really ought to have been the first chapter. The truths here are foundational, and the usual order is to pour the foundation first. But sometimes circumstances preclude this. In this instance, the things that need to be said here are perhaps a tad too radical to put in an early chapter. But now that you are almost done with the book, and there can be no great harm for you in finishing it, I can speak with a little more liberty than I could when we first got acquainted.

The Father is the forgotten member of the Trinity. Jesus we know—He lived among us, and we have read the accounts of His life. The Spirit dwells with us, and although we don't know Him as well as we do Jesus, we do have a sense that He is present. Among conservative believers, among Christians who believe the Bible, there are movements that emphasize a personal relationship with Jesus—the evangelicals, for example. There are movements that emphasize the Holy Spirit—the charismatic movement. But among conservative believers, what movement emphasizes the *Father*? Right. There isn't one. We have a vague notion that liberals used to talk a lot about the Fatherhood of God, and look what happened to *them*.

Evangelicals emphasize "knowing Jesus Christ," or having "a personal relationship with Jesus Christ." In evangelism, it would not be at all uncommon to hear evangelicals asking if someone would like to know Jesus Christ. Nobody asks if anybody would like to know the Father. But one of the distinctive features of the three persons of the Trinity is that they won't let you get to know them alone. They don't allow themselves to be isolated that way. They are constantly introducing us to the other two. The Spirit glorifies Jesus, and Jesus is the way to the Father. It is not possible to meet the Spirit, and cut Jesus and the Father out. It is not possible to meet Jesus, and not be brought to the Father (John 14:6). There have always been boneheaded attempts to separate them, but God will have none of it. To deny the Son is to deny the Father. To receive the Son is to receive the Father (1 John 2:23).

Christians who understand what God is like, and what He is up to, will behave in a similar way. They are constantly moving from one to the other and back again. The early father Gregory Nazianzen once expressed the spirit of the thing gloriously, when he said that as soon as he conceived of the One, he was brought back to the Three. No sooner did he meditate on the distinction between the Three than he was brought back to the One.[1]

The triune God will not allow Himself to be parceled out or divided. My father once told me of a time when I was a small boy, and he had given a copy of Corrie ten Boom's *A Prisoner and Yet* to a Jewish woman who lived in our neighborhood. My father was bringing Corrie to Annapolis to speak, and this woman was a member of an orthodox synagogue there. She was very excited by the book and arranged for Corrie ten Boom to speak at her synagogue. My father accompanied her to the synagogue, and as he listened to her talk, two things occurred to him. The first was that if Corrie said "the Lord Jesus Christ" one more time, they weren't going to make it out of there. The second was that she was clearly filled by the Spirit—because the Spirit loves to talk about Jesus.

"For through him [Jesus] we both have access in one Spirit to the Father" (Eph. 2:18). Think of it this way. The Son is the road. The Father is the city we are driving to, and the Spirit is the car. We are going to the Father, the Son is the way we are to go, and the Spirit enables us to go. Who needs a road that goes nowhere? Who needs a city that no one can get to? Who needs a car when there is no road, and no destination at the end of it? When we are being biblical, we never exclude any member of the Godhead from our thoughts.

But because of our (sinful) tendency to try to think of the persons of the Godhead separately, we can't answer the most basic questions. What is God the Father *for*? As the apostle Paul might say, I know I am out of my mind to talk like this, but the question bears repeating. This is not because the question has no answer (for it obviously does), but pressing the question brings into high relief the fact that *we* don't know the answer. And because we don't know what the Father is for, we don't know what fathers are for. The Father is *for* His own glory, and His own glory is named Jesus, and Jesus was anointed by the Spirit of glory to be the glory of God the Father. Is this divine megalomania? That question would be worth asking if God were not triune, but in revealing Himself as He has, the word *megalomania* is the last word that comes to mind.

What the Father Is Like

So here is a foundational question: What is God the Father *like?* Over the years, I have heard my own father talk about an assignment he has given (countless times) to victims of our father-hungry generation. Suppose that someone is converted to the Christian faith, and he wants to be a good husband and father. He thinks of it as a good thing, and so he is all for it. The only problem is that *his* father ditched when he was only two, and he doesn't have a good grasp of what fatherhood is even supposed to look like. My father has often told young men and women in this kind of position to read through the gospel of John, taking special note of everything that is said about God the Father. We learn what tangible fathers are supposed to be like by looking to the intangible Father. And we look to Him by looking at Jesus, the One who brings us to the Father. If you will bear with me for just a few pages, we can walk through just a small portion of what John reveals for us. There is enough here for us to spend a lifetime unpacking it, but there is also great edification to be found in just a survey.

The Son reveals the Father's glory, a glory full of grace and truth (John 1:14). The Son is the revelation of the invisible Father, a revelation straight from the Father's side (1:18). Zeal for anything associated with the Father's honor consumed the Son (2:16–17), which means the Father is honored above all. The Father reveals Himself to the Son in words (3:34). The Father is generous and openhanded (3:34–36). Because it proceeds from love, this is not an absentminded largesse. It is *generosity*. The Father seeks out worshippers (4:23–24), true-hearted worshippers. The Father works (5:17). The Father works as an exemplar for His Son (5:18–23). The Father trusts His Son, and turns tasks over to Him (5:18–23). The Father seeks honor for His Son (5:18–23). The Father ties His reputation together with the reputation of His Son (5:18–23).

The Father is life essential (5:26), and He shares this life with

His Son to possess in the same way. There is an essential consistency between the Father and the mission given by the Father to the Son (5:36–38). To miss His witness is to miss Him (5:36–38). The pretense that coming in the Father's name could just be another human con job is revealed in this—if it *had been* just another con job, people would have accepted it (5:43–45). The Father is willing to hear the testimony of Moses against his ostensible disciples (5:45).

The Father set His seal on the Son of Man (6:27). The Father is a giver of bread from Heaven. He gave the manna in the wilderness, and He gave Jesus, the ultimate bread (6:32). The Father gives the elect to the Son, and does so irrevocably (6:37). The Father gives the elect to the Son, along with instructions on what to do with them (6:38). The will of the Father is to give eternal life to anyone who looks on the Son with true faith (6:40).

The Father draws people to Jesus (6:44). The Father teaches those whom He draws (6:44–46). The Father is invisible to all except the Son (6:46). The Father is described as the living Father (6:57), and as the source of the Son's life. Consequently, anyone who feeds on Christ has the life of the Father as well (6:57). The Father gives the gift of coming to Jesus (6:65). The Father bears witness to the Son (8:16–19). To know Jesus is to know the Father (8:16–19).

The crucifixion of Jesus would in a unique way reveal His person and mission, and what He had been saying about the Father (8:27–29). The Father bestowed His own authority on Jesus, teaching Him just exactly what to say (8:27–29). The Father accompanied the Son, and did not leave Him alone (8:27–29). The Son consistently did the things that were pleasing to the Father (8:29). Sons imitate their fathers, always, but the Son spoke of what He had *seen* with His Father, while the Pharisees simply did what they *heard* about from theirs (8:38).

The Father gives love for the Son to everyone who is His son (8:42). He sent the Son to earth (8:42). The Son, by honoring His

Father, shows us the Father's honor (8:49). The Father glorifies Jesus (8:54). The Son knows His own in just the way that He and the Father know one another (10:14). The Father loves the Son in His willingness to lay down His life (10:14–18). The Father granted authority to the Son, both to die and to rise (10:14–18). The Father makes Himself known in the works He gave Jesus to do (10:25–26).

The Father protects those He gave to Christ (10:28–32). To be in the hand of Christ is to be in the hand of the Father, because Christ and the Father are one (10:28–32). The Son displayed many good works that were from the Father (10:32). The Father consecrated His Son before sending Him into the world (10:36). The Father and the Son indwell each other (10:38), which can be plainly seen through the works Jesus did (10:36–38).

The Father listened to Jesus (11:41). The Father stands ready to honor anyone who serves the Son (12:25–26), and this service entails following Christ wherever He goes. The Father will ensure that the one who despises his own life in doing this will keep his own life eternally (12:25–26). The Father glorified His name in the life of Jesus, and would glorify it again in the death of Jesus (12:27–28). The Son was under authority in all that He taught, and what He taught was the commandment of eternal life (12:49–50).

The Father intended for the Son to return to Him (13:1). The Father entrusted all things into the hands of the Son (13:3–4). The Father has a spacious mansion, and room for great hospitality (14:1–2). The way to the Father is through Jesus (14:6–7). To know Jesus is to know the Father (14:7). To see Jesus is to see the Father (14:8–13). The Father and the Son indwell each other (14:8–13). The Father does His works by dwelling in Jesus. Once Jesus has returned to the Father, the Father will continue His work in those who believe in Jesus (14:8–13). Answered prayer glorifies the Father through the Son (14:13).

The Father gives the Helper to Christ's disciples (14:16–17). As the Son indwells the Father, so believers indwell Christ, and Christ indwells them. The one who loves Christ will be loved by His Father (14:18–21). Those who manifest a love for the Son by keeping His Word, the Father will also love (14:22–24). Both the Father and Son will come to that person and make themselves at home. The word of the Father is spoken by means of the words of the Son (14:22–24).

The Holy Spirit will be sent by the Father in the name of Jesus (14:25–26). The Son returning to the Father was an occasion of great joy for those who loved the Son (14:28–31). The Father is greater than the Son (14:28–41). The Son proved to the world that He loved the Father, and He did this by letting the ruler of this world have his way with Him (14:28–41).

The Father is the vinedresser of the Jesus vine, and He both prunes and excises branches (15:1–2). The Father is glorified by fruitful believers (15:8–9). We are to abide in Christ, keeping His commandments, in just the same way that Christ abode in His Father, keeping His commandments (15:8–9). The Father's secrets were shared through Christ with the disciples (15:15–16). The Father will hear any request presented in Jesus' name (15:15–16).

To hate the Son is to hate the Father (15:23–24). The Son will send the Holy Spirit from the Father (15:26). The Spirit proceeds from the Father. Demented religious service offered to God is offered precisely because men have not known the Father (16:2–3).

The Spirit will convict the world of righteousness because Jesus went to the Father (16:8–11). The Father and Son share everything (16:15). The Father gives what is asked in Jesus' name, and the principal gift is joy (16:23–24). Believers will be ushered into a direct relationship with the Father (16:25–28). The Father will receive the Son back into Heaven (16:28). The Son was always accompanied by the Father (16:32). The Father and Son glorified each other in the death of the Son (17:1). The Father and the Son shared a pre-creation glory to which the Son was going to return (17:5). The Holy Father would keep, in His own name, those He had given to the Son, so that they could share among themselves the unity that the Father and Son had (17:11).

All Christians throughout history may share in the unity between the Father and Son, such that the world might believe. The Father's glory given to the Son has in turn been given to believers. Christ is in them, and the Father is in Christ, that they might become one, with the world coming to know that God sent the Son, and that the Father loves these believers (17:20–26). The Son desires to bring believers into the glory. The point is to make the Father's love known to the world (17:20–26).

In the context of all this love and glory, the cup of death that Christ was given to drink was a cup of death given to Him by His Father (18:11). After the resurrection, the Son ascended to the Father, to His brother's God, and to His God (20:17). Just as the Father sent the Son, so also the Son sent His disciples. And as the Father had given the Spirit to Him, so also the Son gave the Spirit to His followers (20:21–22).

A Mine Full of Diamonds

This is a mine full of diamonds, and it is hard to know how to carry them all out. And once we have gotten any one of them out, there appears any number of ways to cut it. How can we summarize this? There are no doubt many ways to do this, but it seems to me the most obvious feature of the Father of Jesus Christ is *His generosity*. He is generous with His glory (1:14), with His tasks (5:18), with His protection (10:28–32), with His home (14:1–2), and with His joy (16:23–24). The Father *gives* (3:34–36). The Father gives His Son (3:16; 18:11); the Father gives His Spirit (14:16–17); the Father gives *Himself* (14:22–24).

Learning this about the Father who is a Spirit, who is intangible, should stir us deeply. He is seeking worshippers who will worship Him in Spirit and in truth—in short, who will become like He is. And what is He like? He is generous with everything. Is there anything He has that He has held back? And what should we—tangible fathers—be like? The question is terribly hard to answer, but not because it is difficult to understand.

The great Puritan Thomas Watson once said, "In [Christ] there is the exact resemblance of all his Father's excellencies. The wisdom, love, and holiness of God the Father, shine forth in Christ."[2]

Christ images the Father, and we are to image Christ. The way to do that is clearly to be open-handed. Thomas Smail says this about how we confess our faith when the Spirit moves our tongues.

> If we look in the New Testament for a connection between the work of the Spirit and our relationship to the Father, we shall find it in the letters of Paul. He mentions more than once two confessional cries that are the immediate result of the operation of the Spirit in the lives of members of the Church. The first is *Kurios Iesous*, Jesus is Lord (1 Cor. 12:3), which, he says, can be meaningfully said only *en pneumati hagio*, in the Holy Spirit: the other is *Abba, ho Pater*, Abba, Father (Rom. 8:15; Gal. 4:6). . . . What constitutes the body of Christ is its relationship to and its confession of the Spirit to create the relationship and prompt the confession.[3]

But what happens when the Spirit moves fathers to confess their faith with their *hands*? We began by noting that fathers are called to provide and to protect. The hands of fathers are there for provision (which means openhanded giving), and also to protect. For the former we may read through the gospel of John again and see what the Father has done with His hands—He gives and gives again. For the latter, we can look at the hands of Christ and see the nail prints still.

Questions to Consider:

1. Why is the Father the forgotten member of the Trinity?
2. What person of the Trinity do evangelicals tend to emphasize?
3. What illustration may we use to describe Trinitarian prayer?
4. In your own words, summarize John's description of the Father in his gospel.
5. What are a father's *hands* for?

Chapter 15

It Starts with You

Each chapter has ended with a short list of questions to consider in order to help fathers take spiritual inventory. Every man should seek to determine the impact he is having in his home, and if the questions help, that is great. But at the same time, the questions should not be handled in a wooden or clunky fashion.[1] Wisdom doesn't work that way. The questions and answers are both to be received as a gift of God—lest any boast, lest any despair.

As we conclude, I want to urge men to embrace the high calling of fatherhood. Pick it up and put it on, like a coat. We have looked at a number of particular issues related to the responsibilities of fathers, and it is likely that a number of readers have felt simultaneously encouraged and overwhelmed. As you look at the small faces around your dinner table, you may be discouraged because you grew up without a father, or perhaps you are the first believer that your family ever heard of. Is it too late for you? No. God always takes us from where we are, not from where we should have been. It is not too late for you to be the first in a long line of faithful fathers.

Concerning George MacDonald, C. S. Lewis once said, "An almost perfect relationship with his father was the earthly root of all his wisdom. From his own father, he said, he first learned that Fatherhood must be at the core of the universe. He was thus prepared in an unusual way to teach that religion in which the relation of Father and Son is of all relations the most central."[2]

I am fond of saying that the task for Christian fathers is not simply to get their kids to conform to "the standard." The task, in its fullness, is to bring up kids so that they *love* the standard. But this always needs to be fleshed out. Whenever you are compensating for something, it is always perilously easy to overcompensate. If you are spinning your tires in the right ditch, if something catches, you may well find yourself in the left ditch, nose down. When a culture has walked away from parental authority, and particularly from paternal authority, it becomes easy to assume that the only thing necessary is to somehow reassert that authority. But the point is to *reestablish* that authority, not to simply reassert it. A mere reassertion is a dogmatic claim, to which an unbelieving audience can say, "Yeah, right." And it is always made more complicated when the unbelieving audience is made up of the kids.

As was shown earlier, authority flows to those who take responsibility. Taking responsibility is the foundation of all true authority. This means that reestablishing authority is accomplished by taking responsibility. Often a simple reassertion of authority is an attempt to evade taking responsibility. The point is reasserted so that someone *else* will do what needs doing. This is not only impotent; it is counterproductive.

There are three levels here. The first is when fathers have abdicated their responsibilities, on paper and in practice. The second is when fathers reclaim the authority that is rightfully theirs on paper. They read a book that says fathers should carry the responsibility for the home, and this resonates with them. So they tell everybody that this is what they are now doing—"here are the verses, what's your problem?"—and yet, unfortunately, it turns out that nobody *else* around there read the same book. Or, if they did, they didn't care for it. They say, summarizing the views of Dorothy Parker, that this was not a book to be lightly set aside. It should be thrown with great force.

But the third level is when a father realizes that his fatherly responsibilities need to be reestablished—or not—in the presence of God. This is not something that happens at a dinner table conversation. It is not something that happens because the biggest male in the house screws up the courage to say, "Children, obey your parents" (Eph. 6:1), jabbing at that unfortunate verse with his finger. They might reply, if they have been reading Ephesians lately, "Fathers, do not provoke your children to anger" (6:4). When we are pointing at verses, why do we always pick the ones that the *other* person should be obeying?

In Deuteronomy, we are treated to an obscure law that prohibits boiling a baby goat in its mother's milk (14:21). What is the point of *that*? The principle is clear: if God has given something that is designed for the nourishment of life, that thing should not be transformed into an instrument of death. There are many things that this principle applies to—education, worship, discipline, to name a few—but it most certainly applies to a father's authority. A father's authority was given for life, not for death. For example, the apostle Paul said that his apostolic authority was given to him for building up, not for tearing down (2 Cor. 13:10). It is the same kind of thing with fathers. This is authority that is designed for giving, not an authority for grasping and grabbing. It is authority to sacrifice on behalf of another, not an authority to claim tribute from those others.

So when a father has been given authority, this should be handled by him as his children's *life*. He is not to take that authority, fill a black cauldron with it, and then cook the kids in it. But unfortunately, this is what happens when fatherly authority is merely asserted and enforced, and not lived out in a way as to make it winsome in the eyes of all his children. When a father is confused in this way, he can start to think the most outrageous things. "Well, if the kids don't want to be cooked in it, then they must hate milk. But the Bible says they should love milk."

A father should not want bare conformity. He should want the hearts of his children. This is the plea we find driving the wisdom of Proverbs (23:26). He pleads with his son to give him his *heart*. He is not asking for a grudging, external obedience.[3]

So if loving the standard cannot be accomplished by someone with a loud voice demanding that everyone love the standard, how can it be done? The answer is that this is actually a vertical transaction. If a father believes that it is *God* who has given him this responsibility, then what he needs to do is take up this responsibility before God—*coram Deo*. It is not consistent to believe in God when He is writing the verse that you are buttressing your authority with, but then to not believe in Him when it comes to trusting Him to actually establish your authority. The temptation is to say, "What good would *that* do?" The answer is that God would bless it. If God has no power to establish a father's authority, then what makes us think He would have authority to make rules about it and put them in a book?

We see an example of this in Job. Here was a godly father who took responsibility for what his *grown* children *might* have done in their *hearts*.

> And when the days of the feast had run their course, Job would send and consecrate them, and he would rise early in the morning and offer burnt offerings according to the number of them all. For Job said, "It may be that my children have sinned, and cursed God in their hearts." Thus Job did continually. (Job 1:5)

What did this affect? What did this do? Well, among other things, it brought God to brag about Job to Satan three verses later. This is something Job did before God, and God saw it. God owned it. When we don't do this, it illustrates that we do not actually believe in Scripture. What we are doing is using Scripture on others. Since the Bible is widely respected as an authority by many, we point to verses that establish our position (on paper), in an attempt to manipulate others into some sort of outward compliance. In this spirit, Ambrose Bierce once defined a Christian as someone who believed the New Testament was a divinely inspired book, admirably suited to the spiritual needs of his neighbor.

But if I *believe* that God has assigned to me the responsibility for my wife and children, then I can take up that responsibility before Him, and I can do this without anybody else having to know about it. A father can conduct these transactions with his Father in secret, and his Father who sees in secret will reward him openly (Matt. 6:6). No one might see you change gears, but they *can* see that the car changed speeds. One of those open rewards is the grace of an honored authority in the home, one who is able to bring up children who love the standard.

In other words, a father should be a father in the presence of God *first*. He should assume the mantle of that identity as assigned to him, and he should gladly take it on. Who he is before God is antecedent to what he does—*being* comes before *doing*.

All Christian living, including the part of Christian living that we call parenting, is supposed to be based on this reality—being before doing. The perennial temptation is to try to scrap our way into being by dint of sheer, hardscrabble doing. That is the death trap that the Bible calls "works." If the Holy Spirit of God reverses the order, being first and then doing, that is what we call "grace." Note that when grace is given, the doing doesn't go away. It actually *does* a lot more. Grace gets more doing done than doing does.

Gracious saints work hard; indeed, they work harder than anybody. But they do not trust in their works *at all*—they trust in the grace that God has given.

> Therefore, my beloved, as you have always obeyed, so now, not only as in my presence but much more in my absence, work out your own salvation with fear and trembling, for it is God who works in you, both to will and to work for his good pleasure. (Phil. 2:12–13)

God works it in, and we work it out. The gracious Christian father does not refuse to work. He works all right. He just doesn't try to work it *in*. All our covenant duties need to be approached in this way. We don't earn the salvation of our kids, for example. We don't earn well-adjusted kids. We don't labor to merit high-performance kids. God *gives* our children to us. One of the great tasks of our sanctification is to seek God's aid in finding that works-generator in the basement of our hearts and disconnect that damned thing. I know that for those in the grip of a works trap, this seems like gibberish. They want to know what to *do* to get out of the works trap, and because they want to escape *that* way, the trap stays shut.

So ask the Lord, knowing that if the request is granted, it was granted by giving you the ability to ask aright. That, too, is grace. Fear the Lord and ask Him for what is most needful. This appears elusive. It seems like a great mystery, but it is a mystery that God offers to solve in your life. "The friendship of the Lord is for those who fear him, and he makes known to them his covenant" (Ps. 25:14).

The secret is grace. Not grace *words*, but grace. The covenant is grace. Not grace talk, but grace. And all is given, truly given, through the death, burial, resurrection, and enthronement of Jesus

Christ. The secret of the Lord is before you, on an open palm. What do you do to take it? You believe, and to do that, you have to be one who believes. And to be that, God has to give it to you through the gospel of Christ.

True religion is always found in the presence of God. False religion is always practiced with at least one eye on man, and Jesus teaches us that whether the man is someone *else* is immaterial. Some keep one eye on the mirror.

> Beware of practicing your righteousness before other people in order to be seen by them, for then you will have no reward from your Father who is in heaven.
>
> Thus, when you give to the needy, sound no trumpet before you, as the hypocrites do in the synagogues and in the streets, that they may be praised by others. Truly, I say to you, they have received their reward. But when you give to the needy, do not let your left hand know what your right hand is doing, so that your giving may be in secret. And your Father who sees in secret will reward you. (Matt. 6:1–4)

This entire chapter of Matthew emphasizes the presence and knowledge of the Father. He is mentioned twelve times here, and the structure of Christ's teaching is built up around this truth. Nothing is outside His gaze; everything must be consciously done in His presence. But everywhere we go, we are also in the presence of *men*. And the temptation is to remember them and forget the Father.

The teaching here *assumes* that the followers of Christ will be giving alms. The neglect of this duty has encouraged the statism we now live under, just as the current statism discourages a godly concern for the poor. But we are to be *Christians*, that is, responsive to the Book, and not the current political state. This means that the question concerns *when* we give alms, not *if* we give alms. And the fact that we don't call it alms-giving anymore should not slow us down or deter us. We should be helping the poor financially.

Christ also addresses the question of true rewards. It sounds very spiritual to say that "Christianity should be lived out for its own sake." It *sounds* spiritual, but it is very unspiritual. Christ here positively *requires* His followers to be ambitious for the kind of reward given by the Father. But, He also teaches, this reward is denied to all those who are showboating or grandstanding in front of men. So it is not *whether* we shall have a reward; it is *which* reward we shall have. Seeking a reward from men and seeking a reward from the Father cannot coexist.

But this includes the tricky question of self-reward. There are many individuals who despise those who seek to draw applause from others—such behavior is "tacky." People with greater social skills know how to draw attention to themselves from a watching world in a subtle manner. And if that is insufficient, then we keep an internal ledger whereby we may applaud ourselves. The point of Christ's teaching is not that *you* are the only one who knows. His requirement is that the *Father* must keep the books; *He* should be the only one who knows. As for you, your right hand should not know what your left hand is doing. You do not keep the books.

The Lord teaches us about secret charity and open reward. Returning to the earlier point about rewards, there is nothing wrong with a believer seeking an open reward. The one requirement is that it be left in the hands of the Father. One who is motivated by a selfish ambition *cannot leave it there*. In the same way, we must practice our deeds of charity—in this case, toward our children—in a cryptic, secret manner. How good we are at this should be withheld even from ourselves. This is a godly form of "self-deception." Remember the story Jesus tells about the great day of reckoning (Matt. 25:31–40). Of course, Christ is teaching and requiring *humility*, not absentmindedness. In short, we should seek to be as secretive as we would like the Father to be open in His reward.

And this means that everything comes down to whether we believe our Father. Only one thing is sure—if we believe Him, then He will give us what He has promised.

Appendix

Father Hunger: An Economic View of Delinquent Fathers

Prepared by Economic Modeling Specialists, Inc.

1: Introduction

The climbing number of unwed mothers, the number of fathers in prison, and the ever-expanding divorce rate is continuing to generate significant amounts of research and analysis in the area of family dynamics. According to the National Center for Health Statistics, four in every ten babies were born to unwed mothers in 2007, with historic data suggesting that the number would continue to rise.[1] The purpose of the current analysis is to provide a brief look at the possible economic implications delinquent fatherhood is having on an already battered economy. Because of data constraints, our analysis reflects all children growing up without a father net of those whose father is deceased.

This analysis will not look at the social burden that delinquent fathers place on society due to their increased utilization of social services and correctional facilities (see Scafidi [2008]). Rather, we will look at the long-term fiscal impacts these fathers are having on their children.

TABLE 1: HISTORIC OUT-OF-WEDLOCK BIRTHS AND FATHERLESS CHILDREN

Year	Total Births ('000)	Total Births to Unwed Mothers ('000)	Out-of-Wedlock Birth Rate	Number of Children without Fathers ('000)*
2000	4,059	1,347	33%	19,142
2001	4,026	1,349	34%	18,382
2002	4,022	1,366	34%	18,637
2003	4,090	1,416	35%	19,112
2004	4,112	1,470	36%	19,497
2005	4,138	1,527	37%	19,919
2006	4,266	1,642	38%	19,923
2007	4,316	1,715	40%	18,631
2008	4,247	-	-	19,064
2009	4,136	-	-	19,261
2010	-	-	-	19,700

*** INCLUDES CHILDREN LIVING WITH NEITHER PARENT AND CHILDREN LIVING WITH MOTHER ONLY (NET OF WIDOWED MOTHERS).**

Sources: U.S. Census Bureau, 2011 Statistical Abstract; U.S. Census Bureau, Current Population Survey

We will analyze the children of delinquent fathers by first linking the average education level of these children to future income streams and seeing how these differ from children growing up in traditional two-parent homes. The resulting earnings differential will then be run through an input-output model to capture the associated ripple effects, and a simple with-and-without analysis[2] will be conducted.

Table 2 simply shows the breakdown of the 19.7 million children by family type. The row labeled "Married spouse absent" would include military mothers whose spouse may be called to active duty. Though we recognize that these fathers are not necessarily delinquent, we were unable to disaggregate that figure. The second to last row labeled "No parent present" captures children growing up with grandparents, those in foster care, et cetera.

TABLE 2: 2010 BREAKDOWN OF CHILDREN WITH DELINQUENT FATHERS

Family type	Description	Children
Living with mother only	Married spouse absent	1,073,000
	Widowed	624,000
	Divorced	5,316,000
	Separated	2,727,000
	Never married	7,543,000
Living with neither parent	No parent present	3,041,000
Total number of children with delinquent fathers	(net of children with widowed mothers)	19,700,000

Source: U.S. Census Bureau, "Living Arrangements of Children Under 18 Years (2010)"

Through the advent of more advanced database management software, longitudinal data sets are becoming more widely available. Nonetheless, many of these data sets do not have the requisite variables for providing a comprehensive analysis. Most published data sets have a two-year lag in reporting, which is why much of the current analysis will focus on the problem as it was, not in terms of where we are today. Our intention is to use the data and research that are available, but wherever data are lacking, conservative assumptions will be identified and implemented.

2: Economic Methodology

Total costs of delinquent fatherhood would appropriately capture the loss in productivity and the social burden placed on taxpayers. For research focusing on the social costs of delinquent fathers, see McCord and McCord (1958), Wells and Rankin (1991), and Scafidi (2008). The aforementioned studies focus primarily on the increased burden to society through the increased need for social programs and the generational effect family life has on children. Our focus, however, is on the fiscal impacts, that is, the lost earnings and reduced productivity of the workforce due to delinquent fathers.

We begin with data from the National Longitudinal Survey of Youth. As shown by McLanahan (1999), children from one-parent homes are 16 percent more likely to drop out of high school. We conservatively assume that students from either single parent or two-parent families who do finish high school will persist through the remainder of the education system at comparable rates. Table 2.1 below shows the educational attainment levels of children from one-parent versus two-parent homes.

TABLE 2.1: EDUCATIONAL ATTAINMENT FOR CHILDREN IN ONE- AND TWO-PARENT HOMES

Education Level	One-Parent	Two-Parent
< HS	29.0%	13.0%
HS	35.5%	43.5%
Some College	14.3%	17.6%
Vocational	12.0%	14.7%

Education Level	One-Parent	Two-Parent
Associate's	7.0%	8.5%
Bachelor's	1.5%	1.8%
Master's	0.5%	0.6%
Professional	0.1%	0.1%
Ph.D.	0.1%	0.1%

Source: McLanahan (1999); U.S. Census Bureau, "Survey of Income and Program Participation"

Based on these data, we calculate that the average years of education for a child growing up in a one-parent home is 11.5 years, as opposed to a child in a two-parent home, who has an average 12.1 years of education. Though this difference causes only a minor income disparity between children in one- and two-parent homes, the total effect is quite large when the number of children is taken into account. Obviously, both individuals will be making less upon entrance into the job market and more at retirement age, but the earnings difference throughout their careers is significant. Using the well-tested Mincer earnings profile, we calculate the average annual earnings of a child from a single-parent home to be $31,535, while the child from the two-parent home can expect $34,682. Moreover, the earnings gap between the two also grows over time, as is seen in Table 2.2.

TABLE 2.2: EARNINGS PROFILES AND DIFFERENCES

Year	One-Parent	Two-Parent	Difference
1	$14,386	$15,551	$1,165
2	$15,563	$16,847	$1,284
3	$16,795	$18,207	$1,412
4	$18,081	$19,630	$1,549
5	$19,420	$21,113	$1,694
6	$20,807	$22,654	$1,847
7	$22,240	$24,249	$2,009
8	$23,715	$25,894	$2,180

Year	One-Parent	Two-Parent	Difference
9	$25,226	$27,585	$2,358
10	$26,770	$29,315	$2,545
11	$28,340	$31,079	$2,739
12	$29,931	$32,871	$2,940
13	$31,535	$34,682	$3,147
14	$33,145	$36,506	$3,361
15	$34,754	$38,333	$3,579
16	$36,353	$40,155	$3,801
17	$37,936	$41,963	$4,027
18	$39,492	$43,747	$4,255
19	$41,013	$45,498	$4,485
20	$42,491	$47,205	$4,714
21	$43,916	$48,859	$4,943
22	$45,281	$50,450	$5,169
23	$46,576	$51,968	$5,392
24	$47,793	$53,403	$5,609
25	$48,925	$54,746	$5,821
26	$49,963	$55,988	$6,025
27	$50,901	$57,122	$6,220
28	$51,733	$58,138	$6,406
29	$52,451	$59,031	$6,580
30	$53,053	$59,794	$6,741
31	$53,532	$60,421	$6,889
32	$53,887	$60,909	$7,022
33	$54,114	$61,254	$7,140
34	$54,211	$61,453	$7,241
35	$54,179	$61,504	$7,325
36	$54,016	$61,408	$7,392
37	$53,726	$61,166	$7,440
38	$53,308	$60,778	$7,470
39	$52,767	$60,248	$7,481
40	$52,106	$59,579	$7,473

Year	One-Parent	Two-Parent	Difference
41	$51,331	$58,777	$7,446
42	$50,445	$57,846	$7,401
43	$49,456	$56,794	$7,337
44	$48,370	$55,627	$7,256
45	$47,195	$54,353	$7,158
46	$45,938	$52,982	$7,044
47	$44,607	$51,521	$6,914
	Nominal	$237,428	
	PV	$82,927	

Using a derivative of the earnings profile developed by Mincer, the above table shows the future income stream of a child, assuming he or she enters employment at age 18. The first column in Table 2.2 shows the given year of workforce engagement. Columns two and three show the earnings profile of an individual with 11.5 years and 12.1 years of education, i.e., the earnings of someone growing up in a single-parent home and two-parent home, respectively. The final column shows the difference in earnings by year. Table 2.1 shows the growing gap graphically.

At the bottom of Table 2.2, we show the nominal earnings change and the present value of that earnings change. The nominal earnings figure sums the earnings gap for each year of the individual's working life, and as is shown above, a child raised in a two-parent home will make $237,428 more over the course of his or her life. However, because a dollar today is more valuable than a dollar tomorrow, we discount the future dollars to account for the time value of money. We apply a 4 percent discount rate, standard for long-term investments such as education. After applying this discount rate to the nominal $237,428, we find that the lifetime earnings loss for a child growing up without a father has a present value of $82,927. Multiplying this value by the 19.7 million children with delinquent fathers[3] results in a total *present value* cost of $1.6 trillion, or an average annual cost of $34.8 billion.

Because we link earnings to output, it is worth noting that these lost wages may be thought of as a measure of reduced Gross Domestic Product (GDP), resulting in a lower average productivity rate for the nation's labor force. So far, we have only discussed the direct loss in earnings and national output. Based on the average propensity to consume (APC) in the United States, roughly 95 percent of these lost earnings would have been spent to purchase goods and services. Again, this is a conservative measure, since the less affluent tend to spend larger percentages of their income in consumption rather than investment. Since the APC for the nation includes investors, the 95 percent understates the APC for the average individual under analysis.

To calculate the effects of lost spending, we multiply the 95 percent APC by the average annual lost earnings ($34.8 billion), which results in lost spending of just under $33 billion. This spending would have generated income for employees in other sectors of the economy, which would have caused additional spending. These multiplier effects can be measured through the use of specialized input-output models (for more information on input-output analysis and EMSI data see www.economicmodeling.com). Table 2.3 below shows both the direct and indirect, i.e., multiplier effects, associated with the lost earnings from children with delinquent fathers.

TABLE 2.3: AVERAGE ANNUAL DIRECT AND INDIRECT LOSSES RESULTING FROM DELINQUENT FATHERHOOD

	Labor Income	Non-Labor Income	Total Value Added
Direct	$34,758,855	-	$34,758,855
Indirect	$20,243,232	$5,051,129	$25,294,361
Total	$55,002,087	$5,051,129	$60,053,216

Source: EMSI Analyst: Input-Output Model

Table 2.3 breaks out the impacts between labor and non-labor income. Labor income is that portion of impacts generated through earnings, while non-labor income is income generated from dividends, interest, and rent. Though the direct average annual earnings loss is $34.8 billion, the total loss once accounting for multiplier effects results in an average annual impact of $60 billion, roughly 0.43 percent of the nation's total annual GDP.

3: Conclusions

Delinquent fatherhood has a significant and negative impact on the U.S. economy. There are 19.7 million children in the United States today who are growing up in single-mother homes (net of children with widowed mothers). Though this number slightly overstates the number of children with delinquent fathers, since it captures some children with military fathers on active duty, the overall figure demonstrates the growing generational problem. Children with delinquent fathers receive, on average, 11.5 years of education. Readers may rightly infer that the majority of these children will not graduate from high school, while their peers growing up in a two-parent home are more likely to. Individuals with lower education levels tend to receive lower incomes. The total average annual loss in productivity represents a $34.8 billion loss to the national economy each year. After accounting for associated ripple effects, the total economic loss to the United States as a whole is $60 billion per year.

Notes

Chapter 1: First Words

1. The speaker was Rob Rayburn, at a conference we were doing together in Sandestin, Florida, sometime earlier in this millennium. No idea what year it was.
2. Mike Wilkerson, *Redemption* (Wheaton, IL: Crossway, 2011), 51.
3. Ibid., 52.

Chapter 2: What Fathers Are For

1. "When such attempts don't work, which they haven't, we careen off in another direction. So our egalitarian age is currently insisting, for some reason, that we now learn to respect 'diversity,' but it can give no coherent reason, given its relativistic premises, why we should do so. Without confidence in God's creation design, we have no reason to respect anything, much less diversity" (Douglas Wilson, *Federal Husband* [Moscow, ID: Canon Press, 1999], 33). I have written before on a number of the topics addressed in this book, but rather than quote myself in the body of the text, which would be most unseemly, I decided to put any such references into the endnotes. Those interested in the topic may then pursue it further.
2. Richard Phillips, *The Masculine Mandate* (Orlando, FL: Reformation Trust, 2010), 80.

3. Ibid., 8.
4. Ibid., 12, 14.
5. Q. How many feminists does it take to change a light bulb? A. That's not funny!
6. "In the hierarchical and biblical view, the relationship of women to men is first familial, and then as a consequence, a larger (and very complex) cultural and societal relationship between the sexes emerges. This means that wives are to submit to, and provide help to, their own husbands (and no one else). As a result of this submission in countless families, a larger patriarchal society will in fact emerge. However, this patriarchal society will necessarily contain a number of women who are far more intelligent, educated, and 'stronger' than numerous individual men. No society is truly patriarchal unless it contains a significant number of noble women, stronger in many ways than a number of the men" (Douglas Wilson, *Federal Husband* [Moscow, ID: Canon Press, 1999], 63).
7. Wilson, *Federal Husband*, 63.
8. Because egalitarianism resents this limitation, it takes refuge in various forms of relativism. This relativism asks "who's to say" that we cannot be both this and that. "The gods of synthesis, the gods of gray and off-white, the gods which sidle up next to a man in order to whisper devotional encouragements to him, are altogether something else. These lords of compromise, these gods of soft counsel, *are dangerous*" (Wilson, *Federal Husband*, 71).
9. John Martineau, ed., *Quadrivium* (New York: Walker & Co., 2010), 44.

Chapter 3: A Culture of Absenteeism

1. David Blankenhorn, *Fatherless in America* (New York: HarperCollins, 1995), 1.
2. Jonathan Edwards, "Discourse on the Trinity" in *Writings on the Trinity, Grace, and Faith*, vol. *21* (New Haven, CT: Yale University Press, 2003), 131.
3. Jonathan Edwards, *Works of Jonathan Edwards, vol. 21*, "Writings on

the Trinity, Grace, and Faith" (New Haven, CT: Yale University Press, 2003), 118.

4. C. S. Lewis, *The Lion, the Witch and the Wardrobe* (New York: Macmillan, 1950), 171–72.
5. Richard Phillips, *The Masculine Mandate* (Orlando, FL: Reformation Trust, 2010), 87.

Chapter 4: Masculinity, False and True

1. George Gilder, *Men and Marriage* (Gretna, LA: Pelican Publishing Co., 1986), x–xi.
2. For those who want to pursue this question further, see Brian Mitchell, *Women in the Military* (Washington, DC: Regnery Publishing, Inc., 1998).
3. George Gilder, *Men and Marriage* (Gretna, LA: Pelican Publishing Co., 1986), xi.
4. Steven Goldberg, *Why Men Rule* (Chicago: Open Court, 1993), 228.
5. "Before taking a road trip, it is a very good idea to have some idea of where you are going. Before rearing a son to be 'masculine,' it is equally important to have some notion of what that is. . . . Manhood is where boyhood should be aimed" (Douglas Wilson, *Future Men* [Moscow, ID: Canon Press, 201], 13).
6. "There are two basic directions a boy can take in departing from biblical masculinity. One is the option of effeminacy, and the other is a macho-like counterfeit masculinity. With the former, he takes as a model a set of virtues which are not supposed to be *his* virtues. With the latter, he adopts a set of pseudo-virtues, practices which are not virtues at all" (Douglas Wilson, *Future Men* [Moscow, ID: Canon Press, 2001], 19).
7. "The opposite problem to effeminacy is that of embracing, enthusiastically, a truncated view of masculinity, what I call counterfeit masculinity. This problem 'glories' in masculinity, but has a view of it that no wise observer should consider glorious at all. There is more to masculinity than grunting and bluster. . . . True masculinity

accepts responsibility, period, while false masculinity will try to accept responsibility only for success" (Douglas Wilson, *Future Men* [Moscow, ID: Canon Press, 2001], 22).

8. Richard Phillips, *The Masculine Mandate* (Orlando, FL: Reformation Trust, 2010), 44.
9. "Men gather together in small groups in order to learn how to relate to one another on a more intimate level. In other words, they gather together to learn to relate to one another as women relate to each other. 'Real' masculinity is described as being sensitive, open, responsive, intimate, caring, and the rest of it. (About the only thing missing is breast implants.)" (Douglas Wilson, *Federal Husband* [Moscow, ID: Canon Press, 1999], 37).
10. C. S. Lewis, *God in the Dock*, "Priestesses in the Church?"
11. This is just one of many examples of how, when women try to compete with men, they are abandoning their essential femininity, a femininity that does not measure everything in terms of a competition. "Because one of the male strengths is simple-mindedness, men tend to evaluate all things according to the sort of criterion (fixed in their minds sometime in junior high) best illustrated by arm-wrestling contests or a footrace. Life is simple—stronger and faster is better. And because life is also a contest, everyone is measured by whether or not he or she is 'winning' it. Unfortunately, more than a few foolish women have been sucked into this mindset. And ironically, we call this attempt by some women to be more like men 'feminism,' which is more than a little bit like calling an attempt by cats to be like dogs *felinism*" (Douglas Wilson, *Federal Husband* [Moscow, ID: Canon Press, 1999], 33).
12. "Much of the effort being expended on masculine renewal today is nothing more than a discipleship program for weenies—a pale copy of the secular men's movement of a few years back. In contrast, a husband must assume a mantle of strength and the demeanor of masculine leadership. . . . As the church is reformed in this way, it

will have its former and long-forgotten strength restored. And then a biblical pattern will finally be displayed that may be safely imitated in the civil realm. But until then, all attempts at cultural reform are nothing but 'all pigs fed and ready to fly'" (Douglas Wilson, *Federal Husband* [Moscow, ID: Canon Press, 1999], 76).

13. "This can, of course, be easily misunderstood. No one is saying that a boy with a severed limb should be yelled at for bleeding on the carpet. Nevertheless, instilling toughness in boys is extraordinarily important. A masculine toughness is the only foundation upon which a masculine tenderness may be safely placed. Without a concrete foundation, thoughtfulness, consideration, and sensitivity in men [are] just simply gross" (Douglas Wilson, *Future Men* [Moscow, ID: Canon Press, 2001], 87).
14. But of course I am not arguing that women do not have to be Christian disciples, that they do not have to take up their cross and follow Christ. All of us have to do this, but the differences between the sexes mean that the *form* that cross takes will be different.
15. George Gilder, *Men and Marriage* (Gretna, LA: Pelican Publishing Co., 1986), 14.

Chapter 5: Atheism Starts at Home

1. *Clever Scholars' Review, vol. XIV, no. 6* (East Toad Flats, AR: Air Puff Press, 2025).
2. Friedrich Nietzsche, *The Gay Science* (New York: Vintage, 1974), section 125.
3. Thomas Smail, *The Forgotten Father* (Grand Rapids: Eerdmans, 1980), 56.
4. C. S. Lewis, *Surprised by Joy* (New York: Harcourt, Brace & World, 1955), 115.
5. Paul Vitz, *Faith of the Fatherless: The Psychology of Atheism* (Dallas, TX: Spence Publishing Co., 1999), 13–14.
6. "A father should never fall into the trap of thinking that anything

that is 'strict' is biblical. Most false religions are strict. If a man applies discipline wrongly, he can mess with his kid's head for life. He must not confuse house rules with God's rules. He must teach his children to make such basic distinctions. God does not require that little kids keep their feet off the couch. This is a house rule. God does require that children obey their parents. This is God's rule. And that is why they must keep their feet off the couch" (Douglas Wilson, *Federal Husband* [Moscow, ID: Canon Press, 1999], 99).

7. C. S. Lewis, *The Pilgrim's Regress* (Grand Rapids: Eerdmans, 1933), 59.
8. N. D. Wilson, *Notes from the Tilt-a-Whirl* (Nashville: Thomas Nelson, 2009), 99. If you have ever struggled with the problem of evil, you really need to read this entire book.
9. Christopher Hitchens and Douglas Wilson, *Is Christianity Good for the World?* (Moscow, ID: Canon Press, 2008), 55.

Chapter 6: The Education Axle

1. "Werner Jaeger, in his monumental study of *paideia*, shows that the word *paideia* represented, to the ancient Greeks, an enormous ideological task. They were concerned with nothing less than the shaping of the ideal man, who would be able to take his place in the ideal culture. Further, the point of *paideia* was to bring that culture about. To find a word of comparable importance to them, we would have to hunt around for a word like 'philosophy.' To find a word of comparable importance in our culture, we would have to point to something like 'democracy.' The word *paideia* was as central to the thinking of the Greeks as the idea of the proletariat is to a Marxist, or cash to a televangelist. It was not a take-it-or-leave-it word like whatever the original Greek word for shoelaces was" (Douglas Wilson, *The Paideia of God* [Moscow, ID: Canon Press, 1999], 11).
2. Werner Jaeger, *Paideia: The Ideals of Greek Culture*, vols. *I–III* (Oxford: Oxford University Press, 1939).
3. "If we bring this down into the present in order to illustrate what it

would mean to us, *paideia* would include the books on the bestseller lists, the major newspapers, the most popular sitcoms and networks, the songs on the top forty lists, the motion pictures seen by everyone, the architectural layout of most suburban homes, and, out at the periphery, the fact that all our garden hoses are green" (Douglas Wilson, *The Paideia of God* [Moscow, ID: Canon Press, 1999], 11).

4. Westminster Confession of Faith 3.1.

Chapter 7: Small Father, Big Brother

1. This is why a man "should teach his children the loveliness of pregnancy. Our generation has a pathological hatred of the womb, as evidenced by our abortion culture's imbecility with regard to children. The alternative understanding should be set forth in Christian homes where a man honors his wife with child, her waiting breasts full of grace thinly disguised as milk" (Douglas Wilson, *Federal Husband* [Moscow, ID: Canon Press, 1999], 35).
2. "When our Supreme Court made its infamous decision to all the slaughter of infants, the Christians of our nation were so covenantally blind that we did not see it for what it was—the abortion of the covenanted family. This is not to minimize in any way the horrific nature of the abortion carnage itself; God is just and He will judge. But why did we not even see the other problem? Consider the result of this decision. When a woman is considering an abortion, the Court informed us that this is a decision between her and her doctor. As far as our civil order is concerned, whether she is married or not is completely irrelevant. Whether she has a covenant head or not was not worth considering. The fact that a man has taken a solemn vow assuming covenantal responsibility for his offspring was judged by our highest court to be a matter of no legal consequence. It is difficult to understand what is more tragic, the decision of the Court to slaughter the children or the inability of modern Christians to even notice that the Court had declared every child in the nation to be,

as far as they were concerned, a covenant bastard" (Douglas Wilson, *Federal Husband* [Moscow, ID: Canon Press, 1999], 75).

3. George Gilder, *Men and Marriage* (Gretna, LA: Pelican Publishing Co., 1986), 171.
4. Ibid., 188.
5. Ibid., xii.
6. Ibid., 164.
7. Kathleen Parker, *Save the Males* (New York: Random House, 2008), 195.
8. G. K. Chesterton, *Brave New Family* (San Francisco: Ignatius, 1990), 143.
9. Paul Vitz, *Faith of the Fatherless: The Psychology of Atheism* (Dallas, TX: Spence Publishing Co., 1999), 140.
10. Thomas Smail, *The Forgotten Father* (Grand Rapids: Eerdmans, 1980), 16.
11. G. K. Chesterton, *What's Wrong with the World* (San Francisco: Ignatius, 1910), 43–44.
12. For a fruitful discussion of some of these issues, see Victor Lee Austin, *Up with Authority* (New York: T & T Clark, 2010).

Chapter 8: Escaping the Pointy-Haired Boss

1. John Medaille, *Toward a Truly Free Market* (Wilmington, DE: Intercollegiate Studies Institute, 2011).
2. Joel McDurmon, *What Would Jesus Drink? A Spirit-Filled Study* (White Hall, WV: Tolle Lege Press, 2011), 126–27.
3. Ann Douglas, *The Feminization of American Culture* (New York: Alfred Knopf, 1977), 74.
4. For those who want to study this essential subject further, I highly recommend Gene Edward Veith, *God at Work* (Wheaton, IL: Crossway, 2002).
5. Dave Harvey, *Rescuing Ambition* (Wheaton, IL: Crossway, 2010), 14.
6. Ibid., 31.
7. Ibid., 71.

8. Ibid., 72.
9. Ibid., 102.
10. Ibid., 117.

Chapter 9: Poverty and Crime at the Head of the Table

1. George Gilder, *Men and Marriage* (Gretna, LA: Pelican Publishing Co., 1986), 85.
2. Ibid., 34.
3. Benjamin Scafidi, "The Taxpayer Costs of Divorce and Unwed Childbearing," Institute for Marriage and Public Policy, 11–12.
4. Ibid., 9
5. Ibid., 5.
6. Jonathan Kay, *Among the Truthers* (New York: HarperCollins, 2011), 170–72.
7. EMSI, "Father Hunger: An Economic View of Delinquent Fathers," 6. This study can be found in the appendix.
8. George Gilder, *Men and Marriage* (Gretna, LA: Pelican Publishing Co., 1986), 65. Our problems with this in America are often glibly correlated with race because our pathologies in this regard are overwhelmingly in the black population. But we need to look past the symptoms to the cause—this has all happened because of our lunatic welfare policies, cooked up and administered by bureaucratic dunderheads, themselves being about as white as it gets. And when you apply the same lunatic policies to a white population you get largely the same sort of result. Who could have predicted *that*? See Theodore Dalrymple, *Life at the Bottom* (Chicago: Ivan R. Dee, 2001).
9. Kathleen Parker, *Save the Males* (New York: Random House, 2008), 197.
10. Theodore Dalrymple, *Life at the Bottom* (Chicago: Ivan R. Dee, 2001), 5.
11. "And this is why it is absolutely *essential* for boys to play with wooden swords and plastic guns. Boys have a deep need to have something

to defend, something to represent in battle. And to beat the spears into pruning hooks prematurely, before the war is over, will leave you fighting the dragon with a pruning hook" (Douglas Wilson, *Future Men* [Moscow, ID: Canon Press, 2001], 16).

12. "We fell into sin as a race because we were beguiled by a dragon (Gen. 3:1). God promised to send a warrior who would crush the seed of that serpent (Gen. 3:15), and He has done this in Jesus Christ. In sum, the gospel is the story of a dragon-fight. The serpent of Genesis is the dragon of Revelation (Rev. 20:2), and we are called to rejoice that the dragon has been slain. In contrast, we have reduced the gospel to four basic steps toward personal happiness, and we are much farther from the truth than our fathers were when they told their glorious stories. This is another way of saying that dragon-lore is truer than therapy-speak" (Douglas Wilson, *Future Men* [Moscow, ID: Canon Press, 2001], 102).
13. Richard Phillips, *The Masculine Mandate* (Orlando, FL: Reformation Trust, 2010), 18.
14. Ibid., 60.
15. See Nancy Wilson, *Why Isn't a Pretty Girl Like You Married?* (Moscow, ID: Canon Press, 2010), and Debbie Maken, *Getting Serious About Getting Married* (Wheaton, IL: Crossway, 2006).
16. George Gilder, *Men and Marriage* (Gretna, LA: Pelican Publishing Co., 1986), x. This important book is a revision of his earlier work *Sexual Suicide* (New York: Quadrangle, 1973).
17. Steven Ozment, *When Fathers Ruled* (Cambridge, MA: Harvard University Press, 1983), 174.
18. Horace Bushnell, *Christian Nurture* (Cleveland, OH: The Pilgrim Press, 1994), 328.

Chapter 10: Church Fathers, Ha

1. "Looking for flourishing chastity in such settings is a sexual snipe hunt. Just ask the question directly. Those denominations that

worked through the controversy of women's ordination a generation ago have certainly moved on. Their controversies *now* concern whether sodomites should be wearing sodomitres in solemn procession up the central aisle" (Douglas Wilson, *Why Ministers Must Be Men* [Monroe, LA: Athanasius Press, 2010], 23).

2. "Clearly, women may not be elders or ministers of the word. No matter how much modern exegetes huff and puff, they cannot blow the verse down [1 Tim. 2:11–15]" (Douglas Wilson, *Federal Husband* [Moscow, ID: Canon Press, 1999], 64).
3. "Depending on the issue and the text, liberals are sometimes more to be trusted with the message of the text than conservatives are. This is because liberals are not stuck with the results of their exegesis the way conservatives are. Because conservatives confess that the teaching of the text is normative, the conservative has to make a show of actually doing whatever he comes up with. The liberal can say that the apostle Paul prohibited women teaching in the church—ho, ho, ho—but there it is. At least we get an accurate summary of what Paul's position was. The conservative cannot afford to say that Paul was wrong, and—because whether or not they admit it, conservative churches are pressured by the zeitgeist too—he cannot afford to act as though Paul was simply straight-up right. What to do? What to do? Time for a Greek word study!" (Douglas Wilson, *Why Ministers Must Be Men* [Monroe, LA: Athanasius Press, 2010], 41–42).
4. William Young, *The Shack* (Newbury Park, CA: Windblown Media, 2007).
5. Ibid., 82.
6. Ibid., 90.
7. James K. A. Smith, *Desiring the Kingdom* (Grand Rapids: Baker Academic, 2009).
8. Ibid., 207.
9. Ibid., 126.
10. Ibid., 205.

11. Ibid., 208.
12. Ibid., 210.
13. Here is another example. "Abstention, in this case, is not a matter of seclusion. But neither does it see itself engaged in a triumphalist project of changing the world" (James K. A. Smith, *Desiring the Kingdom* [Grand Rapids: Baker Academic, 2009], 210). In case you were curious, a footnote cites a troubling example of this "transformationist" approach as embodied by Patrick Henry College. I use the word *embodied* deliberately. The folks at PHC actually want to make a real difference, and Smith finds this troubling and triumphalist. It seems that some Christians have gone out on the football field and have allowed themselves to begin to entertain notions of actually winning sometime. This is despite the efforts of the Calvin College cheerleading squad there on the sidelines. "Fight, fight, fight!" (clap) "But don't you dare win!" (repeat)

Chapter 11: Conflicted Feminism

1. G. K. Beale, *We Become What We Worship* (Downers Grove, IL: IVP Academic, 2008), 16.
2. Peter Jones, *The God of Sex* (Colorado Springs, CO: Victor, 2006), 99.
3. C. S. Lewis, *The Abolition of Man* (Toronto: Macmillan, 1947), 35.
4. C. S. Lewis, *A Preface to Paradise Lost* (Oxford: Oxford University Press, 1942), 120.
5. Richard Phillips, *The Masculine Mandate* (Orlando, FL: Reformation Trust, 2010), 60.
6. Ibid., 82.
7. I first heard the illustration from my brother Evan many years ago, but I don't recall when or where. This is what you call your basic "footnote fail."
8. Richard Phillips, *The Masculine Mandate*, 73.
9. Ibid., 72.
10. Ibid., 73.
11. Thomas Smail, *The Forgotten Father* (Grand Rapids: Eerdmans, 1980), 40.

12. G. K. Chesterton, *More Quotable Chesterton* (San Franciso: Ignatius Press, 1988), 182.
13. Kathleen Parker, *Save the Males* (New York: Random House, 2008), 191.

Chapter 12: The Fruitful Father

1. George Gilder, *Men and Marriage* (Gretna, LA: Pelican Publishing Co., 1986), 112.
2. Ibid., 11.

Chapter 13: Some Father Mechanics

1. Steven Ozment, *When Fathers Ruled* (Cambridge, MA: Harvard University Press, 1983), 176.
2. Richard Phillips, *The Masculine Mandate* (Orlando, FL: Reformation Trust, 2010), 93.
3. "Related to this, a wise father rejoices in the fruit of his discipline. This is why many 'disciplinarians' are not disciplinarians in the biblical sense at all. They discipline because they are annoyed or irritated; they are almost impossible to please and they go through life like a crate of crankcase oil. But a 'wise son maketh a *glad* father: but a foolish son is the heaviness of his mother' (Prov. 10:1; cf. 15:20)" (Douglas Wilson, *Future Men* [Moscow, ID: Canon Press, 2001], 28).
4. "A boy who is allowed to drift downward into this sin [laziness] is also being prepared for a life of poverty . . . (Prov. 6:6–11). God does not just promise poverty to this young man, He promises that it will come upon him like a thug with a gun. In the good providence of God, the lazy man is not going to be treated with tenderness. Parents who allow this pattern to develop while their son is under their oversight are asking the providential hand of God to work him over with a baseball bat" (Douglas Wilson, *Future Men* [Moscow, ID: Canon Press, 2001], 60–61).
5. W. Bradford Wilcox, *Soft Patriarchs, New Men* (Chicago: University of Chicago Press, 2004), 106.

6. Kathleen Parker, *Save the Males* (New York: Random House, 2008), 193.
7. Horace Bushnell, *Christian Nurture* (Cleveland, OH: The Pilgrim Press, 1994), 326. I can't quote Bushnell without noting that his effect on theology was in the direction of heterodoxy, and that I consider this to have *not* been a good thing at all. At the same time, his book on Christian nurture is so full of solid good sense on this subject that it simply must be cited.

Chapter 14: Our Father

1. P. Schaff and H. Wace, editors, *The Nicene and Post-Nicene Fathers of the Christian Church: Second Series, Volume 7: Cyril of Jerusalem, Gregory of Nazianzen*, 375, accessed February 24, 2012, http://www.earlychurch.co.uk/readingroom/nazianzus_reading.asp.
2. Thomas Watson, *A Body of Divinity* (Carlisle, PA: Banner of Truth, 1983), 48.
3. Thomas Smail, *The Forgotten Father* (Grand Rapids: Eerdmans, 1980), 30.

Chapter 15: It Starts with You

1. "'*This is a great mystery*: but I speak concerning Christ and the church' (Eph. 5:31–32). Those who want the formation of this great mystery to be reduced to a simple checkoff list want something that cannot be. For those who have no hands, wisdom has no handles" (Douglas Wilson, *Future Men* [Moscow, ID: Canon Press, 2001], 147).
2. C. S. Lewis, *George MacDonald: An Anthology* (New York: Macmillan, 1947), xxi.
3. Richard Phillips, *The Masculine Mandate* (Orlando, FL: Reformation Trust, 2010), 94–95.

Appendix: Father Hunger: An Economic View of Delinquent Fathers

1. http://www.cdc.gov/nchs/data/databriefs/db18.htm.

2. With-and-without analysis simply shows the impact measures occurring under different scenarios. In this case, it compares families in which the father is present with the children, with those in which the father is absent during the upbringing of the child.
3. It is important to note that some children are captured in the data as "living with mother only: married, spouse absent." This category captures children in military families where the father has been called to active duty. To the extent that these children are captured in the analysis, our results will overstate true impacts, since these fathers are not necessarily "delinquent." That said, the number of children in this situation are expected to be small relative to the total number of children being analyzed.

Bibliography

Astone, Nan Marie and Sara S. McLanahan. "Family Structure, Parental Practices and High School Completion." *American Sociological Review* 56, 3 (1991): 309–20.

Blundell, Richard, Lorraine Dearden, and Barbara Sianesi. "Evaluating the Effect of Education on Earnings: Models, Methods and Results from the National Child Development Survey." *Journal of the Royal Statistical Society Series A* 168, no. 3 (2005): 473–512.

Emens, Amie and Jane Lawler Dye. "Where's My Daddy? Living Arrangements of American Fathers." For presentation at the American Sociological Association Annual Meeting. US Census Bureau, August 2007.

Glaze, Lauren E. and Laura M. Maruschak. "Parents in Prison and Their Minor Children." NJC 222984. Washington DC: US Department of Justice, Bureau of Justice Statistics, August 2008.

Grogger, Jeff, and Nick Ronan. "The Intergenerational Effects of Fatherlessness on Educational Attainment and Entry-Level Wages." Bureau of Labor Statistics, US Department of Labor. *NLS Discussion Paper*, no. 96-30 (2003).

Lang, Kevin and Jay L. Zagorsky. "Does Growing up with a Parent Absent Really Hurt?" *Journal of Human Resources* 36, no. 2 (Spring 2001): 253–73.

McLanahan, Sara. "Father Absence and the Welfare of Children." *Coping with Divorce, Single Parenting, and Remarriage: A Risk and Resiliency Perspective.* Mahwah, NJ: Lawrence Erlbaum Associates, 1999.

Scafidi, Benjamin. "The Taxpayer Costs of Divorce and Unwed Childbearing: First-Ever Estimates for the Nation and All Fifty States." Institute for American Values, Institute for Marriage and Public Policy, Georgia Family

Council, and Families Northwest (2008).

______. "Report to Congress on Out-of-Wedlock Childbearing." DHHS Pub. No. (PHS) 95-1257. Hyattsville, Maryland: US Department of Health and Human Services, Public Health Service, Centers for Disease Control and Prevention, National Center for Health Statistics, September 1995.

US Census Bureau. "America's Families and Living Arrangements: 2010." http://www.census.gov/population/www/socdemo/hh-fam.html.

US Census Bureau. "Births, Deaths, Marriages, and Divorces." http://www.census.gov/compendia/statab/cats/births_deaths_marriages_divorces.htm.

US Census Bureau. "Survey of Income and Program Participation." http://www.census.gov/sipp/access.html

Ventura, Stephanie J. "Changing Patterns of Nonmarital Childbearing in the United States." NCHS Data Brief 18. Hyattsville, Maryland: US Department of Health and Human Services, Centers for Disease Control and Prevention, National Center for Health Statistics, May 2009.

Waldfogel, Jane, Terry-Ann Craigie, and Jeanne Brooks-Gunn. "Fragile Families and Child Wellbeing." The Future of Children, Princeton-Brookings. *Fragile Families* 20, no. 2 (Fall 2010).

Wallerstein, J. S. and S. B. Corbin. "Father-Child Relationships after Divorce: Child Support and Educational Opportunity." *Family Law Quarterly* 20, no. 2 (1986): 109–28.

Wildeman, Christopher and Bruce Western. "Incarceration in Fragile Families." The Future of Children, Princeton-Brookings. *Fragile Families* 20, no. 2 (Fall 2010).

Recommended Reading

Bushnell, Horace. *Christian Nurture*. Cleveland, OH: The Pilgrim Press, 1994.

Clark, Stephen B. *Man and Woman in Christ*. Ann Arbor, MI: Servant Book, 1980.

Douglas, Ann. *The Feminization of American Culture*. New York: Knopf, 1977.

Gilder, George. *Men and Marriage*. Gretna, LA: Pelican Publishing, 1986.

Hurley, James B. *Man and Woman in Biblical Perspective*. Grand Rapids, MI: Zondervan, 1981.

Jones, Peter. *The God of Sex*. Colorado Springs, CO: Victor, 2006.

Ozment, Steven. *When Fathers Ruled*. Cambridge, MA: Harvard University Press, 1983.

Phillips, Richard. *The Masculine Mandate*. Orlando, FL: Reformation Trust, 2010.

Piper, John and Wayne Grudem. *Recovering Biblical Manhood and Womanhood*. Wheaton, IL: Crossway, 1991.

Podles, Leon. *The Church Impotent*. Dallas, TX: Spence Publishing, 1999.

About the Author

Doug Wilson is senior pastor at Christ Church in Moscow, Idaho, and senior fellow of theology at New Saint Andrews College. He writes widely on theology, culture, education, and family life in such books as *Reforming Marriage*, *Future Men*, and *Fidelity*.

Index

Scripture References Index

More from Doug Wilson

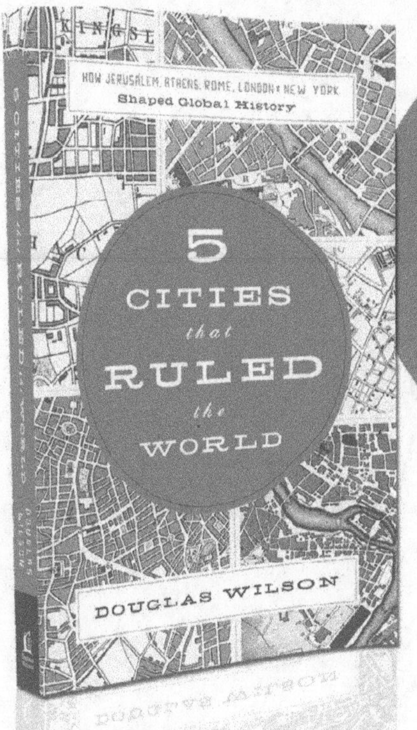

IT'S HISTORY THAT TEACHES US HOPE

In *Five Cities that Ruled the World*, theologian Douglas Wilson fuses together, in compelling detail, the critical moments birthed in history's most influential cities—Jerusalem, Athens, Rome, London, and New York.

Wilson issues a challenge to our collective understanding of history with the juxtapositions of freedom and its intrinsic failures, liberty and its deep-seated liabilities. Each revelation beckons us deeper into a city's story, its political systems, and how it flourished and floundered.

Five Cities that Ruled the World chronicles the destruction, redemption, personalities, and power structures that altered the world's political, spiritual, and moral center time and again. It's an inspiring, enlightening global perspective that encourages readers to honor our shared history, contribute to the present, and look to the future with unmistakable hope.

Available wherever books and ebooks are sold.

thomasnelson.com

9781595554765-A